Tsarist Russia in Greater Syria

Tsarist Russia *in* Greater Syria

Defending Orthodox Interests 1825–1917

Najib E. Saliba

Holy Trinity Publications
Holy Trinity Seminary Press
Holy Trinity Monastery
Jordanville, New York
2024

Printed with the blessing of His Grace,
Bishop Luke of Syracuse
and Abbot of Holy Trinity Monastery

HTSP
HOLY TRINITY
SEMINARY PRESS

An imprint of

Holy Trinity Publications
Holy Trinity Monastery
Jordanville, New York 13361-0036
www.holytrinitypublications.com

ISBN: 978-1-942699-59-0 (paperback)
ISBN: 978-1-942699-58-3 (ePub)

Library of Congress Control Number 2024939761

Cover: Photo, "Emblem of the Imperial Orthodox Palestine Society on Queen Helena Street, the Russian Compound, Jerusalem." Source: Eddie Gerald / Alamy Stock Photo; Map, "Syria: Dead Sea to Mount Sinai, SDUK," 1848. Source: Antiqua Print Gallery / Alamy Stock Photo.

Psalms are taken from A Psalter for Prayer, trans. David James (Jordanville, NY: Holy Trinity Publications, 2019).

CONTENTS

FOREWORD

This concise, but comprehensive book outlining the role the Russian Empire played in Greater Syria prior to World War I (1914–1918) provides valuable historical information to help in understanding both today's geopolitical situation as well as that at the turn of the previous century. Dr Saliba outlines both the political and religious motives behind Russia's protection and patronage of the Orthodox Christians of Greater Syria prior to the abdication of Tsar Nicholas II in 1917, as well as the decline of this patronage after the subsequent fall of the Russian Empire to a godless, atheistic regime that would last a little over seventy years. This patronage, unlike backers of other religious groups such as France and the United States, would insist upon embracing the culture and language of the indigenous people. The result was some of the greatest Arabic writers and poets of the last century, most of whom were Christians. Such people would later spark the Arabic language renaissance and the Pan-Arab movement.

Fast-forward seventy plus years, later after the fall of the Soviet Union and what do we find? We will find that Russia has once again used this historical and religious connection in the Middle East, and especially in modern-day Syria, to protect not only its own geopolitical interests, but the Orthodox Christians of the area as well.

For the United States to fully comprehend the nature of the relationship of Russia with the countries of the Levant, we must fully grasp the importance of the historical and present-day role of Orthodox Christianity in Russia in particular, and the importance of religion in the Middle East in general. While the latter is usually considered by those forming government policy, the former is usually ignored in Washington D.C. altogether. The result is a misguided policy in the Middle East and an unfounded mistrust of all things "Russian." To illustrate this point, just recently when speaking about U.S. policy toward Russia, retired U.S. Army Colonel Douglas Macgregor eloquently said, "This is not the Soviet Union. This is Russia. A Russian State that rests on the foundation of Orthodox Christianity—it's back to what it had been for 1,000 years. We should celebrate that, not destroy it."

Very Rev. Thomas Zain

Chapter 1

Russia's Interests in Greater Syria before World War I

The Historical Connection

The most important interest tsarist Russia had in Greater Syria* before World War I was the security and well-being of the Orthodox Christian Community and unimpeded access to the Christian holy places in Palestine. At that time the Orthodox Christians were the largest of the Christian sects in Syria. Whereas the roots of Christianity in Syria go back to Jesus and his disciples Peter and Paul, Russian Christianity is much younger.

Early conversion to Christianity in Russia occurred in the ninth century A.D., when Photius (c.820–891) was Patriarch of Constantinople. A Christian community with a cathedral was in existence in the city of Kiev in 945 A.D.[1] Christianity gained an even greater following in Russia after the Grand Prince Vladimir I of Kiev (980–1015) converted to Eastern Orthodoxy toward the end of the tenth century A.D. Not only did Vladimir I convert to Eastern Orthodox Christianity, but he also declared Orthodoxy the official religion of

*The term "Greater Syria," known also as "Bilad al-Sham," refers to pre-World War I Syria, before it was divided up and partitioned as mandates by the British and the French in the Treaty of Paris in 1920. In other words, Greater Syria included present-day Syria, Lebanon, Palestine, Jordan, and the district of Alexandretta in northern Syria, which France ceded to Turkey in 1939.

Russia. Hence, a deep spiritual bond was created between the Orthodox Christian communities of Russia and Syria. This bond was destined to grow stronger through time.

The early Russian Church was under the jurisdiction of the Ecumenical Patriarch of Constantinople and led by a metropolitan based in Kiev. The Ecumenical Patriarch appointed and consecrated Russian metropolitans. The Kiev metropolitan assumed the title of "Metropolitan of Kiev and the whole of Russia." Meanwhile, Ivan I assumed the throne of Moscow in 1325, and expanded territorially to annex the city of Vladimir, thus merging the administrations of these two cities. The Kiev metropolitan moved his seat to Moscow which made the city the political and spiritual center of Russia.[2] Ivan I (d. 1340) was backed by the church and so were his successors.

In 1448, five years before the fall of the Byzantine Empire, the Russian Church declared its autonomy, tantamount to independence, from Constantinople. A new metropolitan, Jonas, was consecrated by the Russian bishops. The other Orthodox jurisdictions did not recognize the independence of the Moscow Patriarchate until 1589. It is strongly believed that the transformation of the Moscow Metropolitanate to an independent patriarchate (1589–1590) was positively influenced by the Antiochian Syrian Patriarchate based in Damascus.

Joachim V Daw was the first Antiochian Orthodox patriarch to visit Moscow in 1584. In Russia, he planted the idea that the metropolitan of Moscow should be elevated to the rank of patriarch. It is also believed that he discussed the matter with the patriarchs of Jerusalem, Alexandria, and Constantinople. The idea became a fact in 1589–1590 and the Patriarchate of Rus' achieved parity with other Orthodox patriarchates.[3] The primary reason of Joachim's visit to Moscow was to raise funds to pay the debts his patriarchate owed. He was not disappointed. He met with the tsar and the tsar was generous to him.

Many other Antiochian patriarchs followed in Patriarch Joachim's footsteps. Patriarch Macarius al-Za'im made two trips to Moscow: the first in the 1650s to raise funds, and the second in 1666 to attend the trial of Patriarch Nikon who had a falling out with the tsar. These visits still go on and have strengthened the relationship between the Antiochian and Russian patriarchates. The Russian people view the Patriarchate of Antioch as having seniority over others since its roots go back to Jesus, Peter, and Paul.

Russia: Church–State Relations

Byzantine influences were penetrating Russia well before the fall of Constantinople to the Ottoman Turks in 1453 and the collapse of the Byzantine Empire. More Byzantine influences entered Russia after 1472, when Ivan III (1440–1505) married Zoe Paleologus, niece of the last Byzantine emperor. As Constantinople, the most important Christian city in Europe at the time, breathed its last breath, Moscow began to grow in importance. The grand prince of Moscow assumed the title of "Tsar," meaning Caesar. The prince declared himself the protector of all Christians in the Ottoman Empire. Russia began to model herself after the Byzantine Empire politically, religiously, and culturally. With the rise of Ivan IV (1530–1584), Moscow became the "Third Rome," capital of the only truly Christian empire, and the legitimate heir of the Byzantine Empire, and Moscow "would never fall."[4]

In the Byzantine Empire, the patriarch administered the church and the emperor administered the state. They recognized each other in this capacity and promised to coexist. This dual authority, existing side by side in amity and harmony, did not last. Through time, the emperor gained the upper hand and came to dominate the state and the church.

The same thing occurred in Russia. When Russia was divided politically into principalities, the metropolitan was powerful and could influence the princes. As Russia centralized political power within the hands of one prince or tsar, the metropolitan or patriarch lost power to the tsar. This occurred during the Patriarchate of Nikon and the rule of Fyodor III (1661–1682). Nikon (1605–1681) was of peasant background. He entered church service, had clerical education, and was elevated through the ranks in the church until he became patriarch of Moscow in 1652. As head of the Russian Church, he was strong willed and resolute. He decided to introduce reform and "correct" church books. Traditionalists opposed him strongly, causing a schism in the church known as the Old Believers' Schism which still exists to this day. Nikon also had strong beliefs pertaining to the relationship between spiritual and temporal authorities. He believed that spiritual authority was higher than temporal authority and the tsar should seek the guidance of the patriarch concerning state affairs. Nikon wanted to establish himself as the supreme authority over church and state. This position led Fyodor III to call for a church council attended by the patriarchs of other Orthodox jurisdictions such as Antioch, Jerusalem, Alexandria, and Constantinople. The 1666 church council sided with the tsar. Nikon was excommunicated, demoted, and banished to a distant monastery. Exonerated by Fyodor later on, Nikon died in 1681.[5] Nikon's fate was a severe blow to the authority of the church. Although Nikon was rehabilitated as patriarch following his death, church authority was not. Under Peter the Great (r.1682–1725) the position of patriarch was abolished altogether,[6] a total victory of state over church.

The visits of Patriarchs Joachim V Daw and Macarius III al-Za'im to Moscow established precedents for other Antiochian Orthodox bishops and patriarchs to follow. In 1842, the Patriarch of Antioch Methodius sent Metropolitan Neophytos Halabi of Baalbek, Lebanon, to Moscow to seek financial support. In Moscow, Neophytos was welcomed by Metropolitan Philaret of Moscow (1782–1867) who was a strong supporter of Eastern Orthodoxy in Syria. Metropolitan

Philaret asked the Russian Holy Synod that the Church of the Ascension and Saint Hypatius near the Kremlin be given to the see of Antioch. The Russian Synod and the tsar agreed to this. This is the origin of what became known as the *metochion, amtoosh,* or the Antiochian Representation Church in Moscow that has existed since 1848 to the present day. The word *amtoosh* is derived from Greek, meaning a clerical residence of an independent church located within another independent church or see. It was an equivalent to a "spiritual" embassy that facilitated communications between the patriarchates of Antioch and Moscow. It also facilitated student exchange between Balamand University in Lebanon and Russian theological universities. To return the favor, the Antiochian patriarchate placed St Elias Monastery in Shweir, Lebanon at the disposal of Russian clerics and students.[7] These "representation" churches accelerated charitable donations between Russia and Syria. Notable heads of the Antiochian *amtoosh* in Moscow include Metropolitan Neophytos (d.1853), Raphael Hawaweeny, Alexander Tahan, and currently Metropolitan Niphon Saikaly.

Three Antiochian patriarchs have contributed significantly in strengthening relations between Russian and Syrian Orthodoxy. Two have already been mentioned: Joachim V Daw and Macarius III ibn al-Za'im. The third one was Patriarch Gregory IV Haddad (1906–1928). He was the second Arab patriarch elected to fill that position in modern Syrian Orthodoxy. It has been noted earlier that Peter the Great of Russia abolished the position of patriarch in his quarrel with the church over authority. The first Romanov ascended the throne of Russia in 1613. In 1913, Tsar Nicholas II wanted to celebrate 300 years of Romanov rule. He needed a patriarch to preside over liturgical celebrations. Since the Russian Church had none, Tsar Nicholas extended an invitation to the Antiochian Patriarch Gregory Haddad to come and preside over the celebrations. He accepted the invitation.[8]

Patriarch Gregory left Beirut by ship on his way to St Petersburg. He stopped in Istanbul for a meeting with the Ottoman sultan and his grand vizir, then on to Russia. At St Petersburg, he was received with great jubilation.

Metropolitan Vladimir of St Petersburg welcomed him into the city saying, "I am certain that your visit to Russia will leave in us not only pleasant memories of your beloved personality, but also will always remind us of our spiritual bonds that bind us strongly together."[9] Patriarch Gregory responded saying, "All the people of the East, Slavs, Greeks and Syrians firmly think of the noble duty Orthodox Russia has. Every Orthodox loves Russia strongly, considering her his decent, noble-minded protector… and please note that what impresses us the most is not only Russia's greatness but also her zeal to preserve right worship and real piety."[10]

Patriarch Gregory stayed in Russia about two months. An entourage of metropolitans and clerics accompanied him. On March 6, he presided over the divine liturgy at the Kazan Cathedral commemorating 300 years of Romanov rule. Tsar Nicholas II, his family, and members of their dynasty were present. They exchanged gifts and good wishes. The patriarch presented the tsar with an icon going back to the fifth century A.D., plus a number of religious manuscripts. The tsar gave the patriarch special gold medals struck to commemorate the occasion. Members of the patriarch's entourage also got medals. The patriarch informed the tsar of the needs of his patriarchate and the tsar promised to help.[11] Patriarch Gregory also took advantage of his presence in Russia to visit many churches and accepted donations offered by the Russian people.[12]

After a successful two-month visit to Russia, Patriarch Gregory returned to Syria in June 1913. He was accompanied by a group of Russian clergy who were supposed to establish a Russian Theological Center at St Elias Monastery in Shweir, Lebanon. The Russian clergy, however, were forced to return to their country as World War I broke out and the Turks sided with Germany in that war.[13] In 1917, toward the end of the war, the Bolshevik Revolution occurred in Russia. The anti-church Communists seized power at this time. The Russian Orthodox Church now entered a very dark period during which the church was persecuted, priests imprisoned, and churches were torn down or turned into swimming pools and concert halls. During World War II, the persecution of the church was reduced because Joseph Stalin needed the support of the church to rally the people to defend Russia against the German invasion. The Church's long night finally ended with the collapse of Communism in 1989–1991.

Under Communist rule, communications between the Russian Orthodox Church and the Antiochian Patriarchate were not totally severed. In May 1945, as World War II was winding down, Patriarch Alexi I of Russia led an entourage on a visit to the Middle East. He visited Jerusalem, Egypt, and Beirut.[14] As a result of this visit, a Russian representative church was established in Beirut in May 1946 equivalent to the Antiochian representative church (*amtoosh*) in Moscow. Additionally, a delegation representing the Moscow Patriarchate, headed by the Metropolitan Gregory of Leningrad, arrived in Beirut in November 1946. It is important to note here that Beirut has hosted a significant Russian community whose roots go back to the Bolshevik Revolution of 1917, if not before.

Mention must also be made of the delegation led by the late Metropolitan Elias Kurbān of Tripoli to Moscow in May 1978, representing the Antiochian patriarchate in the celebrations marking the restoration of the position of patriarch to the Russian Church. "There is no need to speak in detail about the strong brotherly relationship which binds the Antiochian see to that of Moscow," Metropolitan Kurbān said. "The relationship is strong, historical and gets stronger with the passage of time," he continued. "It suffices to mention the visit of the Antiochian Patriarch Macarius III ibn al-Za im in the seventeenth century A.D., and that of Patriarch Gregory IV Haddad in 1913, during which he elevated Archimandrite Alexi to the rank of bishop, becoming the Patriarch of Moscow and all Russia later on. We also remember with great appreciation what your church has offered us, past and present by way of help, material, spiritual and educational, which did a lot of good in our beloved Middle East."[15]

Reflecting basically the same spirit was the message sent by Patriarch Alexi II on the occasion of the opening of a symposium on October 19, 1997, at Balamand University titled, "Russia and the Orthodox Christians of the East." Having welcomed the participants in the symposium, the patriarch went on to say that following the collapse of the Byzantine Empire in 1453, Russia became the only independent Orthodox country in the world. For this reason, the hopes and longings of the Orthodox Christians of the East focused on Russia. In those trying times, the Russian people, the spiritual children of Orthodoxy, did what they could to strengthen the position of their brothers in the East. The Orthodox Christians of the East still remain the center of Russia's attention. Russia's material support to the ancient patriarchates in the Middle East was an important aspect of its activity in this area. In exchange, the patriarchs of Constantinople, Antioch, Alexandria, and Jerusalem would visit Moscow bringing sacred objects for safe-keeping.[16]

In the eighteenth and nineteenth centuries, Russia offered brotherly help in religious and clerical developments as well as in improving different aspects of church life. This effort was undertaken by Metropolitan Philaret who was sainted by the Russian Church. At his initiative, representative missions (*amtooshes*) were established in Moscow by the sees of Alexandria, Antioch, and Jerusalem in order to strengthen relations and facilitate communications between them and Moscow. Additionally, the establishment of the Imperial Orthodox Palestinian Society in 1882 is proof of Russia's concern about the well-being of her coreligionists in the East. More than 103 schools were built by Russia in Greater Syria at no cost to the students or to the local people.

One last evidence of the continued communications at the highest level between the two patriarchates of Antioch and Moscow is the invitation Patriarch John X of Antioch received from the Patriarchate of Moscow and all Russia to participate in celebrating the tenth anniversary of the elevation of Patriarch Kirill to the rank of "Patriarch of Moscow and all Russia" which he accepted graciously and fulfilled in late January 2019, leading an Antiochian delegation of clerics and laity.

At their first meeting, Patriarch Kirill welcomed Patriarch John X and his delegation to Moscow as the proof of the strong and deep historical ties that bind them. Patriarch Kirill also applauded the strong role Patriarch John X had been playing in the Antiochian patriarchate and stressed that Moscow and Antioch must cooperate in order to overcome the problems both face. Patriarch Kirill then mentioned the areas in which the two are closely involved, such as repairing and restoring damaged churches and monasteries in Syria.

In response, Patriarch John X expressed his joy and his delegation's joy in being in Moscow to participate in the celebrations. He emphasized the deeply rooted relationship between Moscow and Antioch, not forgetting the problems they both face. He also thanked the Patriarchate of Moscow and the Russian State for their help past and present saying, "Despite problems, Syria today is much better than before; there is more security and stability now. All problems should be solved through discussion and consensus, not war."

Chapter 2

Political, Economic, and Military Interests

The first chapter traced the rise of religious spiritual bonding between the Antiochian Orthodox Christians of Greater Syria and those of Moscow and all of Russia. Although the spiritual bond continues and gets stronger through time, other interests began to develop toward the end of the seventeenth and through the eighteenth and nineteenth centuries, especially during the reigns of Peter the Great (1682–1725) and Catherine the Great (1762–1797). Russia was a land-locked country without significant access to the sea, except in the north which could not be used most of the year because of ice. Russia also had no access to the Baltic Sea in the west because it was a Swedish lake. Peter the Great raised an army, fought and defeated Sweden, and expanded Russia's borders westward to the Baltic coast. He built St Petersburg, named it after himself, and made it his capital—Russia's window on the West. Not only did Peter the Great expand Russia's borders westward, he also changed Russia's orientation. Ever since the Mongol invasion of Russia in the thirteenth century, Russia had turned her back to Europe and faced East. Peter the Great reoriented Russia to the West and initiated a program to modernize Russia on Western lines.

When Peter the Great assumed power, Russia had no access to the Black Sea in the south either. Like the Swedish controlled Baltic, the

Black Sea was an Ottoman lake. The Ottoman Empire also controlled the Turkish Straits, the Bosporus and the Dardanelles, which Peter considered "the keys to the Russian house."[17] Peter expanded Russia to the south, defeated the Ottoman Empire, and seized control of the northern Black Sea coast. Peter's successor, Catherine the Great, continued this policy. She transformed the Black Sea to a Russian lake and opened the Bosporus and Dardanelles to Russian merchant ships, allowing Russian access to the Mediterranean Sea.[18] As "heirs" to the Byzantine Empire, virtually all Russian tsars aspired to control Constantinople and the Straits for religious, economic, political, and military reasons.

Until approximately the end of the seventeenth century, Russia's interest in Greater Syria was purely religious. The first Russian naval presence in the eastern Mediterranean developed as a result of the Russian-Turkish War of 1768–1774. The Ottomans had virtually occupied all Byzantine territory in eastern Europe and western Asia before the fall of Constantinople in 1453. The Byzantine capital had already become an island in an Ottoman sea. As a result of the Ottoman occupation of eastern and southeastern Europe, millions of Christians, including Orthodox Christians, found themselves under Turkish rule. These subjugated Christians rose up from time to time against Ottoman rule and looked to Russia, the only independent Orthodox country left in the world, for help. To help Balkan Christians in the Russo-Turkish War of 1768–1774, Russia sent units of its Baltic fleet westward to the Atlantic Ocean, then southward to the Mediterranean Sea through the Strait of Gibraltar to Greece and the Syrian coast. Russia intended to hit the Ottoman Empire in its "soft underbelly." It landed forces in Greece and besieged ports on the Syrian coast including Sidon and Beirut. Sidon surrendered to the Russians and Beirut was bombarded by the Russian navy until it surrendered. The Russian navy at this time cooperated with some anti-Ottoman rebels. Having occupied Beirut, the Russian navy stayed about five months during which the Russian flag fluttered in Beirut's sky.[19]

The net result of this war was the sound defeat of the Ottoman Empire and victory for Russia. To legally end the war, the two powers negotiated the Treaty of Kutchuk Kainardji of 1774, which considerably enhanced Russia's political and economic interests in the Ottoman Empire. In the treaty, "the Sublime Porte promised to protect constantly the Christian religion and churches, and allow Russian ministers at Constantinople to make representation on their behalf."[20]

Additionally, the treaty stated that "Russian ships would have free passage in the Turkish Straits and Russian merchants would be given 'most favored nation' status. Russia also was given the right to intervene on behalf of the Russian Church to be built in Istanbul."[21] Hence, from 1774 onward, Russia claimed the right to intervene in favor of the Orthodox Christians—the largest and most powerful body of Christians in the Ottoman Empire, numbering about 15 million.[22] Russia also affirmed the Orthodox Christians' right, first obtained in the Treaty of Carlowitz of 1669, to visit Christian holy places in Jerusalem and elsewhere in Palestine without obstruction or tax payment.

The Ottoman-Russian War of 1768–1774 produced other results as well. It was the first active Russian political-military intervention in Syria. It awakened the interests of the Syrian people in Ottoman-Russian relations and paved the way for future interventions. Russia became part of the balance of power game in the Eastern Mediterranean area. Economically, the war enhanced commercial exchange between Russian and Syrian ports.

Russia and the Greek War of Independence

The 1820s witnessed another Russian intervention in the Eastern Mediterranean. The Greeks, having been under Ottoman rule for centuries, rose up against the Ottomans in 1821 in a bloody uprising in which Greeks massacred Turks in Greece, and Turks massacred Greeks in Istanbul. The Orthodox ecumenical patriarch and some bishops were hanged. The Ottoman government, short of military forces to suppress the uprising, called upon Muhammad 'Ali, Ottoman governor of Egypt, to suppress the rebellion. As governor of Egypt, Muhammad 'Ali was successful in building a relatively strong army and navy in Egypt. He responded positively to the Sultan's request, using his navy to transport Egyptian forces to Greece. The Egyptian army did well against the rebels and almost succeeded in suppressing the rebellion. But the Greek rebels were popular in western Europe, which supported them morally and materially. Even the English poet, Lord Byron, volunteered to fight on the rebels' side. Unwilling to see the rebels defeated, three European navies—British, French, and Russian—intervened in 1827 and destroyed Muhammad 'Ali's navy in the Battle of Navarino Bay.

Consequently, Egyptian forces were forced out of Greece. The Treaty of Adrianople (1829), negotiated under Western auspices, legally ended the war. As a result, a small, autonomous (soon to become independent) Greece emerged.[23] This treaty marks the birth of Greek independence still celebrated today. Because Russia's navy was involved, Tsar Nicholas I gained prestige and strengthened his claim as defender and protector of Orthodox Christians in the Ottoman Empire. Peace was restored, but more interventions were to follow.

The Crimean War: 1854–1856

The roots of the Crimean War lie in the unrelenting competition of European Christian missionaries over the guardianship of Christian holy places in Palestine, and especially Jerusalem. They represented many nationalities and religions, including French, English, German, Italian, and Russian. Their objectives were varied, not only preaching the Gospel and teaching how to attain the Kingdom of God. What is important in this context is the strong competition between French and Russian missionaries over the guardianship of Christian holy places in Jerusalem, especially the Church of the Holy Sepulchre. French missionaries were the first to establish themselves in Syria while the Russians were the last. France had been recognized by the Ottoman Empire in treaties, the latest in 1740, that France was the protector of Latin Christians in the East. But, there were hardly any Latin Christians in the East. The Latin Christians came with the Crusaders in 1099 A.D. and were expelled with the Crusaders in 1291 A.D. The overwhelming majority of the Christians in the Ottoman Empire and in Greater Syria were Orthodox Christians who viewed the tsar as the protector and defender of their faith, Orthodoxy. The popular name of Russia was "Holy Russia" and the tsar was the head of state and of the church. As it was in the Byzantine Empire, there was no separation between church and state. Peter the Great had abolished the position of patriarch until it was restored with the election of Patriarch Tikhon on November 5, 1917. In the period when the position was vacant, the Russian Holy Synod administered the church and whenever the Synod met, the procurator (the tsar's representative) attended the meeting and reported to the tsar. In this way, the tsar was head of the church and state combined, and Tsar Nicholas I tried to make the most of his position.

Tsar Nicholas I was aware that the Ottoman Empire was declining and was the first to refer to the sultan as "the sick man of Europe." In a discussion with Sir Hamilton Seymour, British ambassador to St Petersburg, the tsar hinted at the partition of the property of the sick man of Europe.[24] His eyes were focused on Constantinople, which Russian tsars coveted for centuries. The British ambassador disagreed, telling the tsar that "the sick man could be nursed back to life."

Following this encounter with the British ambassador, a Russian envoy was sent to Constantinople demanding certain concessions for the Orthodox Church at shrines in Jerusalem, and recognition of Russia as the protector of Christian Slavs.

In 1852, a dispute arose between the Russian and French representatives at Constantinople regarding the guardianship of the Church of the Holy Sepulchre in Jerusalem. In the meantime, the French ambassador was instructed to remind the sultan of the "unaltered right" of the Catholics in Jerusalem to demand the restitution to the Catholics of the seventeen sanctuaries "usurped" by the Greek Orthodox. The sultan decided in favor of the Catholics. When Tsar Nicholas learned of the sultan's decision favoring the Catholics, he sent Prince Menschikov to the sultan with two demands: the guardianship of the Church of the Holy Sepulchre in opposition to that of France, and a protectorate over members of the Orthodox Church throughout the Ottoman Empire. Supported by the British, the sultan rejected the tsar's demands and declared war on Russia. This was the background of the Crimean War. As the war started, Britain, France, and the Italian State of Sardinia-Piedmont joined the war against Russia. Each of those states had an axe to grind in this war. The fighting occurred in Crimea in southern Russia on the Black Sea. The port of Sevastopol, a fortified Russian naval base, was besieged by the allies but not easy to storm. The siege lasted until September 1855, when the allies finally captured the base at a great cost in human lives. Meanwhile, Nicholas I died in March 1855, and was succeeded by his son Tsar Alexander II. The new tsar inherited a defeat on the battlefield and an exhausted Russia. Rather than continue a hopeless war, the combatants signed an armistice on February 25, 1856, and proceeded to Paris for peace negotiations. In the Treaty of Paris, signed March 1856, Russia renounced its claim to be recognized as protector of all Orthodox Christians in the Ottoman Empire and accepted the neutralization of the Black Sea. This meant total Russian demilitarization of the Black Sea, a significant defeat.

The Crimean War was the most important war between 1815 and 1914. It came close to being a world war. It was noted for its misery, human suffering, and the vanity of war. More soldiers died from disease than bullets. It was also a significant setback for Russia, albeit a temporary one. By 1870, Russia had sidelined virtually all the restrictions put on her in the Treaty of Paris. The effect was similar to that which the Treaty of Versailles (1919) had for Germany at the end of World War I.

Intervention in Syria: 1860

Four years after the Treaty of Paris was signed there was another intervention by Western powers in the eastern Mediterranean, this time in Syria. In 1860, a sectarian war broke out in Damascus and spread to Beirut and parts of Mount Lebanon during which several thousand Christians were killed and thousands fled their homes seeking security elsewhere. Since Syrian Christians, especially Maronites, were favored in the West, some Western powers—like Britain, Austria, and Prussia—asked Louis Napoleon (Napoleon III), the French emperor, to intervene and stop the sectarian war. Napoleon did send several thousand troops to Syria to stop the conflict. By the time they arrived in the eastern Mediterranean, the Ottoman government had intervened, stopped the sectarian war, and punished the perpetrators. Unwilling to see French troops alone in the eastern Mediterranean, Tsar Alexander II dispatched Russian troops to balance the French forces and protect Orthodox Christians. There was no action in this latest intervention besides reinforcing the idea that France was the protector of Papal Christians and Russia the protector of Orthodox Christians. The only tangible result of the 1860 intervention was the establishment of the district of Mount Lebanon—some 2,000 square miles in area, predominantly Christian, autonomous under a Christian governor selected by the Ottoman government and approved by European powers. Mount Lebanon became the foundation of the current 4,000 square miles of the Lebanese republic created by France in 1920 through the annexation of the City of Beirut, South Lebanon, and the Bekaa Valley. Whereas the Mount Lebanon district was predominantly Christian, this Christian majority was largely diluted by the creation of "Greater Lebanon."

Chapter 3

Russian Pilgrims

In many religions, a pilgrimage to holy places is a meritorious act and enhances one's salvation. So it is in Christianity since its early centuries. A good example would be Helena, mother of the Roman Emperor Constantine (r. 306–337) who legalized Christianity in the Roman Empire in the Edict of Milan in 313 A.D. Helena, now Saint Helena, made her pilgrimage to Jerusalem and is said to have found the true cross on which Jesus was crucified. Since then, Christian pilgrims have been converging on Jerusalem from all over the world.

The first known Russian pilgrim who went to Jerusalem was Daniel, a monk and the head of the monastery in Kiev. He led a group of pilgrims in the early twelfth century (1104–1107) to Jerusalem, walking on foot, and wrote a book about his journey, which lasted about two years.[25] Following Daniel's footsteps in the middle of the fifteenth century was the cleric Varsonovy, who visited Syria and Egypt, staying two months in Jerusalem and four nights in the Church of the Holy Sepulchre.[26] A third Russian traveler who spent much time in Lebanon visiting many cities in 1728 was Vasili Grigorovich-Parski, a traveler, writer, and publisher. He traveled widely between 1728 and 1747, visiting countries in Europe, Asia, and countries around the Mediterranean Sea. The city which he visited six times and fell in love with was Tripoli in northern Lebanon. He visited many churches and monasteries—Orthodox and Maronite.[27] He was ordained a priest at the hands of the Antiochian Patriarch Silvestros in January 1734.[28] He wrote a book about his travels calling it *Rihlat* or *Journeys*.

During the reign of Peter the Great (1682–1725), the number of pilgrims going to Jerusalem went down significantly because Peter was quarreling with the patriarch over authority. Peter succeeded in abolishing the position of patriarch, bringing both church and state under his control. In the first decade of the nineteenth century, the situation began to improve and more pilgrims visited the holy places in Palestine. Furthermore, Russia opened a consulate in Jerusalem in 1819 to address pilgrims' problems more efficiently.[29] In the middle of the nineteenth century, a ship line was opened between Odessa on the Black Sea and Syrian ports. Additionally, by the mid-nineteenth century, "Austrian and French shipping companies had been carrying annually several thousands of Orthodox pilgrims to Palestine."[30] Similarly, with the end of the Crimean War in 1856 and the official opening of the Russian Consulate in Jerusalem in 1859, there were more communications and trade between Russia and Syria. Ships, mostly Russian, came regularly from Odessa to Jaffa and other Syrian ports bringing goods, mail, and passengers, especially pilgrims. It is estimated that by the end of the 1850s, ten to twelve thousand Russian pilgrims annually made their pilgrimage to the Holy Land.[31] From the 1860s onward, the number of pilgrims increased steadily from year to year, except during the Russo-Japanese War of 1904–1905 when the number went down temporarily. Some Russian pilgrims would come to Palestine before Christmas and stay until Easter.[32] They would visit the holy places, walking on foot from one place to another. Mikha' il Nu'aimah, a graduate of the Russian Seminar (Teacher's College) of Nazareth, tells us that "the Russian pilgrims used to come to the Holy Land shortly before Easter every year. We used to see them coming to Nazareth in groups of hundreds or thousands walking on foot, with beards or without, men and women, but mostly peasants."[33]

Overall, Russian pilgrims derived from all social classes, but the majority belonged to the peasantry, and women outnumbered men. This fact notwithstanding, some individuals and Western states were fearful and suspicious, considering the Russians' influx to Palestine as a political-economic threat, not simply a manifestation of piety.[34]

The Russian Ecclesiastical Mission in Jerusalem

Reports had been circulating in Russian government offices and among royalty in St Petersburg of Protestant and Catholic missionaries infiltrating Orthodox Christian communities in Greater Syria. They were trying to tempt them to convert to Catholicism or Protestantism by promising them protection, education, and even money. In the early 1840s, memorandums were submitted to Tsar Nicholas I urging him to create a permanent Russian mission in Jerusalem headed by a top cleric to counteract the establishment of an Anglican bishopric and a Latin patriarchate in Jerusalem.[35] The tsar could not ignore this. He was head of state and church at the same time, carrying the title of "defender of the faith and preserver of doctrinal unity." Having asked for advice and reflected on the issue, Tsar Nicholas and the Russian Holy Synod agreed to send a fact-finding mission to investigate the situation in Jerusalem and Greater Syria and report back to St Petersburg. The head of this mission was Archimandrite Porphyry Uspenski (later on Bishop Uspenski), a scholar and writer on Byzantine history, as well as an archaeologist and conservator.[36] As Uspenski was preparing to leave for Jerusalem in May 1843, he was instructed to report about the condition of Russian pilgrims, investigate the activities of Catholic and Protestant missionaries, and also to provide information about the situation within the Orthodox Christian community of Greater Syria.

Armed with these instructions and some money, Uspenski embarked for Beirut in the fall of 1843. He spent about ten months traveling in Christian Orthodox towns and villages to gain an impression of the living conditions. The information he gathered about the state of Orthodoxy was shocking. Poverty, ignorance, corruption, lack of schools, and uneducated priests were the norm. The Greek clerical hierarchy was blamed for this.[37] Part of the blame also went to the wealthy Orthodox because they didn't care about the education of their poorer coreligionists. It is important here to remind the reader that in the Ottoman Empire, each religious community was responsible for the education of its members. There were no public schools open to all, and since top positions in the church were usually occupied by ethnic Greeks, who had no interest in educating Arabs.

Through his investigation, Uspenski confirmed to the tsar and the Russian Synod that the previous reports they had received were true. He sympathized with the Arab population because he cared for the education of young Arab Orthodox Christians. They led a movement in the latter part of the nineteenth century to free the church from ethnic Greek control. They succeeded in the Antiochian patriarchate, but failed in the Jerusalem patriarchate which is still under ethnic Greek control today. His work done, Uspenski returned to St Petersburg in October 1843. Barely a year after his return from Jerusalem, the tsar called upon him, with the approval of the Holy Synod, to head and lead the first Russian Ecclesiastical Mission to the Holy City. His responsibilities were wide ranging.

First, he was to take care of the Russian pilgrims and make sure their stay was as comfortable as possible. In the middle of the nineteenth century, about 2,500 Russian pilgrims visited the Holy Land annually. Second, he was to gain the confidence of the Eastern clergy and support native Orthodox Christians in their struggle against Catholic and Protestant missionary propaganda. In a nutshell, he was supposed to revive Orthodoxy and breathe new life into it—all within a budget of 10,000 rubles annually.[38]

Uspenski performed well under difficult circumstances. His contribution was not only administrative but also intellectual. He wrote the story of his life in seven volumes. He did a lot to improve the quality of Arab life. He was the founder of the ecclesiastical mission in Jerusalem and presided over it until 1853. He was succeeded as head of the mission by Antonin (Kapustin) who also left his mark.

Under Antonin, the mission was transformed from a landless mission to one with vast land ownership within Old Jerusalem, its first near the Church of the Holy Sepulchre. It soon acquired the name of the "Russian Zone," and the home of the Ecclesiastical Mission. It included churches, monasteries, hostels, and other facilities. The following quotation is explanatory:

> Between 1858–1864, the Russians acquired considerable lands in Palestine. They acquired a historical spot near the Church of the Holy Sepulchre. They built a colony in Jerusalem comprised of a hostel which could accommodate 300 males and 600 females (pilgrims), a hospital (60 beds), five domed Cathedrals, a residence for the Russian consul, and a house for the Russian Ecclesiastical mission with a private chapel and accommodations for 80 people.[39]

This complex was consecrated by the Russian Church in 1865.

Chapter 4

The Battle over Greater Syria

All through the nineteenth century, a relentless battle was being fought over the hearts and minds of the people of Syria. The roots of this battle go back centuries in time and include religious, economic, political, and military reasons. The combatants, however, were Western religious missionaries trying to take advantage of a collapsing Ottoman Empire by establishing spheres of influence in the said empire. More specifically, the conflict involved numerous French Catholic missions active in Greater Syria trying to convert Orthodox Christians sympathetic to Russia. This would weaken Russia which had declared itself protector and defender of Orthodoxy in the Ottoman Empire. France and Russia were also at loggerheads in the nineteenth century over the protection of the Christian holy places as well as the few Latin and Roman Catholic Christians in the empire. The majority of the Christians in the empire were Orthodox Christians, more sympathetic to Orthodox Russia than to Catholic France. From the Russian viewpoint, France was an intruder in Syria.

French missionary orders which were active in Syria throughout the nineteenth century when competition peaked included: Franciscans, Capuchins, Jesuits, Carmelites, Lazarists, Cordeliers, and Freres. Members of these orders, although all were French and Catholic, competed strongly among themselves over church services in the French Consulate at Aleppo. The above list is not all inclusive. There were also orders of French nuns with branches in Syria such as: the Sisters of Charity, nuns of the Sacred Heart, and St Joseph's nuns. Some orders of nuns focused on female education and were based in several places in Greater Syria.

French missionaries preceded all others in Syria by about a century and a half. The first Catholic missionary school was established in Bethlehem in the sixteenth century. It was intended to provide pilgrims with translators proficient in French.[40] In the following century, French missionary activity in Syria increased. The number of schools went up to six, offering a variety of courses on Catholicism and other subjects. The most active Catholic missionary Orders included the Franciscans, the Capuchins, Carmelites, and Jesuits. These orders and others opened schools and convents in different places in Syria to teach, preach, and "sell" their preferred religious sect. The Jesuits were the most active of all.[41] They competed strongly for space, students, influence, and converts. Since Muslims, Jews, and Maronite Christians were beyond reach, Catholic missionaries focused on Syrian Orthodox Christians. They were more open-minded, hungry for education, and the least controlled by their clergy.[42] Hence, they became an easy prey as they attended Catholic missionary schools.

The language of communication in French missionary schools was French. Arabic, if taught, was considered a second language. It was not emphasized. At breaks, students sometimes were forbidden to speak Arabic, and if they did were penalized. Hence, graduates of French missionary schools were strong in French and weak in Arabic, more gallicized than Arabized. This class of "Arabs" considered Arabic as a kind of peasant language, while French was considered higher class language. Agafangel E. Krimsky, a nineteenth-century Russian author who lived in Beirut and Mount Lebanon for about two years, relates in his memoirs that "the Arab residents of Beirut, with the exception of the older ones, wear European clothing. But their elegant European look, is only external. Many of them, or rather most of them, chatter in French. This is what a student attending a Jesuit school told me. It is amazing how strong French influence is in Lebanon. People think if you know French, this is equivalent to all there is to know."[43] A.L. Tibawi, a Palestinian scholar basically reached the same conclusion when he said, "Missionary schools are often accused of having produced imitation Europeans, men and women, fascinated with the superficialities of Western civilization without grasping its spirit, aping outward Western manners and showing scant respect for their own tradition."[44]

French missionary orders dominated Syria by establishing schools, universities, hospitals, orphanages, and nunneries while seeking converts and spreading the French language. France supported and protected its Catholic orders financially and morally. The Jesuit Order, for example, was banned in France following the outbreak of the Revolution in 1789. France frowned at Jesuits internally, but it continued to support and protect them externally. How can we explain this contradiction? The book by Agnes de Dreuzy[45] may shed some light on a possible explanation. She writes, "As for France, Palestine was the land where it had the most significant religious responsibility. In addition to the long privileged tradition of protecting the Latin and Eastern Catholic populations, the French as the chief of Catholicism, held a special position in the protection of the Holy Places of Palestine."[46]

The above explanation of France's involvement in Syria sounds hollow in view of the historical facts. Who asked France to assume this religious responsibility in Palestine? Palestine was part of Greater Syria, and Greater Syria was part of the Ottoman Empire from 1517 to 1920. Furthermore, who were the Latin Christians in Palestine and where did they come from? Some Latin Christians came with the Crusaders in 1099 and returned with the Crusaders when they were expelled in 1291. There were a few Eastern Catholics who had seceded from the Eastern Orthodox Church early in the eighteenth century with the help of the French consuls and French missionary orders. The absolute majority of Christians in Greater Syria were Orthodox, and they didn't ask for French protection.

The American Mission to Syria

"Your mission is to be regarded as a part of an extended and continually extending system of benevolent action, for the recovery of the world to God, to virtue, and to happiness."[47]

The quotation above constitutes the objective of the mission articulated by the American Board of Commissioners for Foreign Missions and given to the two American Presbyterian missionaries, Reverends Levi Parsons and Pliny Fisk, who were about to embark for Syria in order to fulfill this mandate. The goal of the first American missionaries to Greater Syria was to convert Muslims, Jews, and the "nominal Christians" to Protestantism. They believed they were paving the way for the return of Christ, ushering in his thousand-year reign. Only Protestants could be saved. The mission of the first American missionaries was not even restricted to Syria; it involved the whole world. The American missionaries were supposed to move eastward to convert the Persians, Indians, Chinese, and so on. The "nominal Christians" were the Christians of Syria who included the Maronites, Melkites, and Orthodox. The American missionaries didn't even know that there were Christians in Greater Syria. They were discovered by accident and were described in unchristian terms. The American missionaries were asked by the American Board to learn Arabic, distribute Bibles, and gather information about the area. In brief, they were to spread the Gospel of Christ and enlighten every non-Christian, or rather non-Protestant they encountered. Toward the closing of the 1840s, two more objectives were added to the original mission: the foundation of a native Protestant Church and the translation of the Bible into Arabic.

When the American missionaries arrived in Syria they thought that Jerusalem would be their base, but once there they had second thoughts. They found it crowded and full of interest groups. Having considered the options, they ended up choosing Beirut as the center of their operations, exactly where the American University of Beirut (AUB) is located today. By the fall of 1823, they had already set up camp there.

From the beginning, the missionaries' method of "recovering the world to God" was through preaching and teaching. The first school opened by the American mission was in Beirut on July 28, 1824. They had seven students with Tannus al-Haddad as their native teacher.[48] The missionary residence served as the school. In the fall, however, a house was rented to accommodate about fifty students. Opposition on the part of the Orthodox students soon surfaced and the Orthodox patriarch prohibited Orthodox children from attending. Some dropped out and others stayed. In 1826, the number of mission schools in Beirut and vicinity varied between six and nine, with some three hundred boys and girls attending. In 1828, the whole American mission in Beirut relocated to Malta, native Americans and converts, because of local insecurity and the war between Russia and Turkey. In the mid-1830s schools numbered ten with about 240 boys and 85 girls; church members numbered nine.[49] Meanwhile, the American mission established two more stations, one in Jerusalem and the other in Bethlehem. The number of missionaries went up to twelve plus two female teachers. In 1846–1847, there were altogether twelve schools with fifteen teachers and 450 students, 150 of whom were girls.[50] Arabic was the teaching language according to the Board for Foreign Missions based in Boston. English was not taught because native customs, manners, traditions, and language were to be maintained and not adulterated.[51]

The decade of the 1840s opened with a war waged by the British and the Ottoman government to expel Muhammad 'Ali, governor of Egypt, from Syria. He ruled Egypt from 1805 to 1849, the year of his death. He had fought for the sultan in Arabia and Greece. In the early 1830s, he turned against the sultan and occupied Greater Syria. This ran against British interests in Syria. Consequently, Britain instigated an uprising in Syria against Muhammad 'Ali in 1840 which forced him out of Syria and back to Egypt. The political instability resulting from this war affected the American mission in Syria significantly. The war forced the mission to relocate to Cyprus and about half of the mission schools closed. The Mission Seminary at Abeih was suspended. Although it eventually reopened, not all the students returned and the seminary lost its vitality.[52]

The 1850s form a watershed in the rise of Protestantism in Greater Syria. At mid-nineteenth century, Butrus Bustani, a convert to Protestantism and an intellectual, established a Protestant Church in Beirut "which included nineteen men and four women."[53] At this time, the mission included seventy-five converts to Protestantism in all of Syria. The mission also had thirty primary schools and approximately 900 students.

The Beirut Church was served by an American pastor. About the same time, Protestantism spread out of Beirut to Hasbaya in southern Lebanon. About fifty formerly Orthodox Christians converted to Protestantism and founded the second Protestant Church in Syria. Unlike the first church in Beirut, the one in Hasbaya was served by a native pastor ordained in 1853.[54] Additionally, three new churches were established at Abeih (1852), Aleppo (1852), and Sidon (1856). Finally, the last important objective fulfilled in the mid-nineteenth century was the translation of the Bible into Arabic.[55] By the closing of the 1850s, the American mission in Greater Syria had a firm foundation. American missionaries numbered fifteen plus a few native assistants. There were also thirty primary schools with about 1,020 boys and girls who were all taught by native instructors.[56] These developments combined with British-American pressure led Sultan 'Abd al-Majid I (r. 1839–1861) of the Ottoman Empire to issue a *firman* (decree) in 1850 recognizing Protestantism as the fourth *millet* (religious community) in the empire after Islam, Orthodox Christianity, and Judaism.[57]

The American mission gained influence and got established as a result of recruiting homeless or neglected people into their schools. They also employed personnel whose reputation was questionable in their original churches. Most likely, employment and a sense of belonging influenced the conversion to Protestantism.[58]

Just when the American mission in Syria was in its best position since its founding, the American Civil War broke out. The American Civil War was disastrous to the American mission in Syria. It terminated the mission's financial support which closed many schools in the countryside. In addition, a sectarian war broke out in Syria in 1860 which pitted Druze against Christians (Maronites). As a result, some 7,000 Christians, including about 100 Protestants, converged on Beirut for security and support, which the mission could hardly provide.[59] Economizing became synonymous for survival. The Board in Boston was reluctant to pay for secular education that prepared young men for worldly pursuits. The Board's dictum was that teaching should complement preaching.

As a result of the American Civil War and the cessation of funds for the mission, Catholic missionaries tried to take advantage of this opportunity by boosting their investments in education in the area. They were partly successful. Anglican missions also tried to fill the void left by the Americans, which led the secretary of the Board of American Missions to describe the intervention of the Anglican Bishop of Jerusalem in Aleppo and elsewhere as "intrusion and breach of courtesy" for encroaching on America's "sphere of influence."[60]

Opposition to the American Mission

When American missionaries first set foot in Syria, they were welcomed by the Maronite and Orthodox patriarchs. The welcome was of short duration. The Maronite Patriarch turned against the American missionaries first and was soon followed by the Orthodox patriarch of Antioch. The Antiochian patriarch forbade Orthodox children from attending American missionary schools.[61] The Maronite and Antiochian patriarchs, especially the former, issued their anathemas against the "Bible Men," as the American missionaries were called, and against all who should receive or retain their books. Everywhere the Americans were branded as "vile heretics."[62] The Maronites strongly resisted the Protestants and threatened anyone who dealt with them with excommunication. As'ad al-Shidyaq was the first Maronite convert to Protestantism and its first victim. He suffered a tragic fate and died in the Maronite patriarch's prison.[63] Some of the difficulties faced by the American missionaries in Syria included "spiritual indifference on the part of the natives," opposition of Eastern Churches, small missionary apparatus, and scantiness of resources.[64]

Orthodox Christian opposition to the American mission peaked in 1836 as Orthodox children were withdrawn from mission schools, Orthodox teachers were prohibited from teaching in mission schools, and religious material distributed by the Americans was burned. The patriarchs of Constantinople and Antioch, together with the bishops and metropolitans signed an encyclical denouncing the Americans as heretics and resolved to protect the Orthodox *millet*.[65] The Orthodox patriarchs were backed by Orthodox Russia. When the American missionaries converted part of the Orthodox of Hasbaya [66] to Protestantism, the Russian Consul lodged a complaint with the Ottoman government, affirming Russia's role as protector of Orthodox Christians in the empire.[67]

Early American missionaries in Syria felt superior to local Christians, calling them "nominal Christians." They were full of "pride, ignorance, superstition, and wickedness." "Even Muslims were morally superior to Eastern Christians."[68] This was truly insulting. The following quotation reflects the haughtiness and arrogance of some mission members, if not all of them:

> In the year 1819, the first American missionaries came to Western Asia, bringing the Gospel of Christ to the Mohammedans, but in their explorations they came in contact with these various oriental Christian sects. They found them to be ignorant, illiterate, superstitious, idolatrous... It is a painful and sickening spectacle to enter a Greek church and see crowds of worshipers burning incense, lighting tapers and bowing before the filthy painted boards, and then devoutly kissing them and crossing themselves... The Greek Church stands condemned from its own authorized symbols as polytheistic, idolatrous, and unscriptural.[69]

The American mission in Syria suffered from several failings. Some of its members were not Christian enough. They came to Syria to preach the Gospel of Christ but they were not good role models to the people they came to Christianize. The mission was opposed to equal native participation in its work—administrative or spiritual. "A native could be a subordinate helper but not an independent equal." Native teachers were barred from the rank of professor at the Syrian Protestant College (est. 1866) until 1895. Natives also were paid less than their American counterparts and race figured in appointments to teaching positions until the end of the Ottoman Empire. Discrimination caused tension between American mission members and Syrian natives. It also caused friction within the American mission itself because some American mission members called for equality between Americans and Syrians. Miss Law was a mission member who was supportive of such equality. While she was on vacation back in the United States, missionary Henry Jessup wrote a letter to the mission center which said, "Miss Law's radical ideas of leveling Americans down and Syrians up are simply impracticable." He recommended that she not return to Syria.[70]

Before 1883, natives could join the college as teachers whether they were Protestants or not. This changed in 1883 when instructors were required to be "not merely members of evangelical churches, but in full sympathy with the spiritual and missionary aims of the college and with the religious doctrines and sentiments of those who direct or support it."[71]

Throughout the nineteenth century, especially the second half of it, the territory of Greater Syria was a battleground among many religious missionaries representing several European states, competing to win the hearts and minds of the Syrian people. French missionaries were the first. They were followed by British, American, Italian, German, and belatedly Russian. All were vying for power and influence. The competition over Syria was the consequence of the progressive weakening of the Ottoman Empire, "the sick man of Europe." The great intellectual Mikha'il Nu'aimah stated, "The Ottoman State has gotten so old and disunited to the point of dissolution. Additionally, the western states, using religion as a cover, started to spread their influence in parts of that collapsing empire. This is the reason we have so many French, English, German, Italian, American and Russian schools in Palestine, Syria and Lebanon."[72] Russia, the protector of Orthodoxy in the Ottoman Empire, established the Imperial Russian- Palestinian Society to spread its influence and language.[73]

The Russian scholar Agafangel E. Krimsky mentions in his memoirs that the town of Shweir in Mount Lebanon has seven schools, four of which are boarding ones. The reason for this is the competition among missionaries. The Protestants established one school, the Jesuits followed and established two schools, the Maronites also established a school, and the Orthodox established three schools.[74]

Finding converts in Syria was the key for influence and prestige. Catholic French missions and Anglo-American Protestant missions competed feverishly for converts to the extent of offering material and other rewards for conversion. When Muslims, Jews, and

Maronites proved to be beyond reach, missionaries focused on the Orthodox Christians.[75] The Orthodox Church lost many members to Catholicism and Protestantism in the last quarter of the nineteenth century. A.E. Krimsky predicted the end of Orthodoxy in Syria within a century. Rewards for conversion included money, trade, protection, education, and employment.[76] All members of the native Protestant Church, about fifteen, were employed by the American mission and materially dependent on it. This was probably what led Rufus Anderson, Secretary of the Board of Foreign Missions, to write a letter to the Syrian mission saying, "We feel strongly in the belief that your mission has erred in affording so much temporal aid in various forms to your converts… If the hold you have on the converts is chiefly mercenary, it will prove like a broken reed. If the state of Syrian society is such that our converts, to be obtained and retained, must be partially or wholly supported by us, we had better go elsewhere…"[77]

The strong rivalry between American Protestant and French Catholic missions led to the establishment of two universities in Beirut. The American mission started preparations to open a college in 1862 which culminated in the opening of the Syrian Protestant College on December 3, 1866. Students numbered sixteen and teachers two—one American and one native. Daniel Bliss served as president. There were two departments, literary and later a medical one which opened in 1867. The objective of the college was to train missionaries and to promote secular disciplines.

The Jesuits were in Syria long before the French Revolution of 1789 and were banned following it. They were reconvened after the fall of Napoleon and returned to Syria about 1831. Although their relationship with the French government internally is somewhat vague, France supported them externally and used them as an instrument to promote French language and culture. Having returned to Syria, they built schools and followed a strong anti-Protestant policy and anti-American mission. They used education to spread their beliefs. The Jesuits opened a school in Ghazir, a town in the Kisrawan district in Lebanon which was transferred to Beirut in 1875 to become St Joseph's Jesuit University.[78] This balanced the Syrian Protestant College, renamed the American University of Beirut (AUB) in 1920. Whereas the AUB distanced itself from its missionary background and became a secular institution dedicated to teaching and *free* inquiry, its counterpart could not do so and continued to believe in France's traditional role as a "civilizing mission" in the world.

Missionary Activity and Imperialism

Is there a link between missionary activity and imperialism? In theory, there shouldn't be because they are two separate activities which are essentially opposed to each other. A missionary is a person in the service of a holy message. His means of communicating with people are peaceful. He preaches a message of love, peace, tolerance, and forgiveness. Imperialism is a totally different activity. It is based on war, territorial expansion, colonialism, and oppression. The two activities are theoretically irreconcilable. However, if we discuss the question posed above with reference to nineteenth-century European imperialism, we may find a link between missionary activity and imperialism. In some African and Asian countries, especially China, the missionary preceded the soldier. The latter followed the former to "provide security." Consequently, China was penetrated by several European countries, plus Japan and the United States, and divided into spheres of influence by the closing years of the nineteenth century. Foreign presence in China finally culminated in the outbreak of the Boxer Rebellion of 1898–1900, an anti-foreign uprising in China. A lot of blood was shed. It took an international force from several European countries, plus Japan and the United States, to suppress the Boxer uprising.[79] (See Appendix 1 for the negative implications of imperialism in the Western hemisphere.)

A.L. Tibawi, a Palestinian scholar, believed that European missionary activity led the way to imperialism and colonialism.[80] Imperial countries sometimes invoked Rudyard Kipling's "The White Man's Burden," or humanitarianism, to justify imperialism. Under the cover of religious missions, first the French, the British the Americans, and others entered Syria and established schools, promoted their own languages, religions, and cultures. They established spheres of influence and turned the native people against themselves. The missionaries discriminated against the natives on the job, in school, and in church. Similarly, at the end of World War I, Britain and France used the League of Nations "mandate system" to divide Syria and Iraq into British and French mandates to justify the expansion of the British and French Empires.

Needless to say, the British and French mandates were no less oppressive and exploitative than direct imperialism which in reality they were. It is not an exaggeration to say that the political instability that has prevailed in the Fertile Crescent (Greater Syria and Iraq) since World War I has been caused, to a large extent, by the political engineering which Britain, France, and the United States of late have done in that part of the world. In the final analysis, the link between missionary activity and imperialism is real and cannot be denied.

The mission given to the American missionaries about to depart for Syria as articulated by the Board of Commissioners in 1819 was "to recover the world for God." How did they do? Did they fulfill their mission? If we interpret the mission given to the American Commissioners literally, and if we judge the commissioners based on their achievement, the answer to the question posed above must be more negative than positive. The American missionaries did not do very well. They fulfilled a tiny part of their mission but not all of it. They converted only a small number of Syrians to Protestantism. They certainly didn't "recover the world for God." In about a century of teaching and preaching, they couldn't convert the Muslims, the

Jews, not even the Maronites and the Catholics. Those whom they could reach and were open to conversion were primarily Orthodox Christians. But why were some Orthodox Christians open to conversion? Was it conviction, employment, money, or education? We do not know for sure. Perhaps education was an important factor. What we know about the Orthodox is that they were more open-minded, more liberal, and less controlled by their clergy, since the top clerics were ethnic Greeks, not Arabs. But how big was the Protestant community of Syria after about a century of missionary work? Not big, perhaps about 5,000 members in all of Greater Syria. When we think of Syrian Christians today what comes to mind is that they are either Orthodox, Maronite, or Catholic Melkites, not Protestants. A contemporary Western writer was very perceptive in commenting on the achievement of the American mission in Syria saying:

> It is, unfortunately, true that the hopes which were entertained ninety years ago, when the Syrian mission was begun [1822], have not been realized. There has been no general awakening to newness of life among ancient churches, and even less among the Mohammedans. Nor has the mission had any deep and abiding effect upon the numerous Maronites, Druzes, Metaavileh and Nusayriyeh.[81]

Chapter 5

Education in Greater Syria

As stated earlier, Syria and much of the Arab World became part of the Ottoman Empire after Sultan Selim I (r. 1512–1520) defeated the Mamluk State based in Egypt (including Syria) in the battle of Marj Dabiq near Aleppo in 1516. Along with the acquisition of Syria and Egypt in 1516, Selim I also acquired the Caliphate from the last Arab caliph based in Cairo. Selim I was the first Ottoman ruler to assume the title Sultan-Caliph in the Ottoman Empire. Hence, the state of education in Greater Syria cannot be discussed separately from the state of education in the Ottoman Empire as a whole.

The Ottoman Empire was religiously organized into *millets,* or religious communities. Every *millet* enjoyed considerable autonomy in the empire under its religious chief. Up until 1850, there were three *millets* in the empire. The first *millet* (based on size) was the Muslim *millet* headed by Shaikh al-Islam, the highest legal authority in Islamic law. The second *millet* was the Orthodox Christian *millet* headed by the ecumenical patriarch in Constantinople (Istanbul).

The third *millet* was the Jewish *millet* headed by the chief rabbi. In 1850, under British-American pressure, Sultan Abd al-Majid I recognized Protestantism as the fourth *millet*. Protestantism became established in the empire as a result of the activities of the Anglo-American Protestant missionaries in the first half of the nineteenth century, but there weren't many Protestants in the empire. Up until the end of the nineteenth century, the Protestants of all Greater Syria probably numbered about 5,000 or less. Since the Ottoman population was religiously organized into *millets* and considered autonomous, the government played no role in the education of its citizens. Every *millet* was responsible for the education of its members. This system continued basically until the last quarter of the nineteenth century when the Ottoman Empire had little time left to live. There was no national education based on a common curriculum that all students had to take regardless of their religion.

In Sunni Muslim schools, a pupil's education began in Katatib, the lowest elementary level, at the hands of a tutor, male or female, known as Khuja. Katatib have deep roots in Muslim history going back to the rise of Islam. In Katatib, boys and girls learned together. They were also known as Qur'an schools where pupils learned *tajwid*, recitation of parts of the Qur'an committed to memory, rules of worship, penmanship, reading, and writing. Students and teacher usually sat on a mat in a house or mosque for their lesson. Mosques always served as schools and houses of prayer and worship under Islam.[82] Sunni Muslim education based on Katatib deteriorated through time reaching its lowest in the middle of the nineteenth century. By this time, according to A.L. Tibawi, no religious community had good education. Schools were few in number, no adequate number of teachers qualified to teach, not enough books, and education was based on rote learning.[83]

Additionally, community schools shared common weaknesses which included few schools, poor quality, limited offerings, and few qualified teachers. Teachers had to do more than one job to earn a livelihood.[84] When Midhat Pasha served as governor of Syria (1878–1880), he altered the way things were done in the province. He improved existing schools and opened new ones; he improved communications, brought fresh and clean water to Damascus; he changed the way of life for the better.[85] For once, Syria had a free press, but when Midhat Pasha was suddenly removed and disposed of, things returned to the way they had been. Under Sultan Abdul Hamid II (1876–1909) schools suffered from censorship; subjects such as history, geography, philosophy, and political science disappeared from the curriculum.[86]

Of all three Christian sects in Greater Syria, the Maronites had the highest literacy rate. The Maronites had eight colleges, two for monks and three general.

Many subjects and languages were taught.[87] Additionally, Constantin Pitkivich, the Russian consul in Beirut, states in his memoirs that every Maronite Bishopric had a school which taught Arabic and ancient Syriac, plus four schools in the Mount Lebanon area noted for theological studies supervised directly by the Maronite patriarch.[88] He went on to say that the Maronites owned more schools in Mount Lebanon than all other sects combined.[89] The Maronites also owned a printing press at Dair Mar Qizhayya where Arabic and Syriac books were printed.[90] George Antonius agrees that of all Christian sects in Syria, "The Maronites were the best educated ... had colleges at Zgharta [in North Lebanon] (1735) and 'Ain Waraqa (1789) ... graduates of 'Ain Waraqa contributed to the revival of learning in Syria."[91] The Maronites also benefited from schools established by French Catholic religious missionaries in the cities, towns, and villages of Syria. This is what helped the French language spread and achieve ascendancy over other languages in the second half of the nineteenth century.

The Melkite Catholics of Greater Syria closely followed the Maronites in promoting educational activity. They originally followed the Orthodox Church but seceded from it about 1725 and established their own patriarchate in 1728. Their most important school, that of 'Ain Taraz, is located in Mount Lebanon and includes a division dedicated to theology. Next in importance comes the Patriarchal College of Beirut which also welcomes non-Catholic students like Orthodox, Muslims, and Jews.[92] Like the Maronites, the Melkite Catholics benefited significantly from the presence of a multiplicity of French missionary schools all over Syria.

As mentioned earlier, the Roman Catholic Church established contacts with Syria in the sixteenth century, but real missionary work started early in the seventeenth century around 1622. Hence, French missionaries had the field to themselves, with no competition until the nineteenth century.[93] French missionaries who built schools and convents included the Jesuits, Lazarists, Capuchins, Franciscans, and others. There were female missionaries as well. Schools established by these missions provided education to many and helped spread French influence and language.[94] France offered annual scholarships to Maronite and Melkite Syrian students to study in French missionary schools.

Scholars agree that Orthodox Christians in Greater Syria formed the majority sect but were behind Maronites and Melkites in educational activity. "It should be noted that the Christian element in the Mountain population with least access to education of any kind was the Orthodox Melkites."[95] The Russian consul in Beirut, Constantin Pitkivich, at about the middle of the nineteenth century, positioned the Orthodox in third place after the Maronites and the Melkites in educational achievements.[96] He blamed in part the Orthodox spiritual leaders for this shortcoming because the Ottoman *millet* system made spiritual leaders, not the government, responsible for the education of their flock. Who were the spiritual leaders of the Orthodox patriarchates of Jerusalem and Antioch? Since the fall of Constantinople to the Ottoman Turks in 1453, the hierarchs of the Orthodox Church in Jerusalem and Antioch were ethnic Greeks and their flock was overwhelmingly Arab. Pitkivich also blamed wealthy Orthodox because they did not provide money to build schools to educate their coreligionists. The Orthodox flock was hungry for education in the nineteenth century. French Catholic and Protestant missionaries took advantage of this by building schools and colleges in Orthodox towns and villages. They lured Orthodox students, males and females, through offering scholarships and other temptations to attend their schools. Once in, Orthodox students became easy prey for Catholic and Protestant missionaries looking for converts. This is how and why the Orthodox Church lost not hundreds but thousands of members to Catholicism and Protestantism across Greater Syria.

As to higher education, there were two alternatives: either the Syrian Protestant College (the AUB after 1920), or St Joseph's University. The former was favored by Orthodox students and some Melkites, the latter was popular with the Maronites and some other Uniates. These two institutions constituted the backbone of higher education until modern times.

The Rise of the Russian Orthodox Palestine Society

The Russian Orthodox Palestine Society was the brainchild of the Russian Orientalist Vasili Nikolaevich Khitrovo. Khitrovo was a strong believer in Orthodoxy. He made his first pilgrimage to the Holy Land in 1871. Following his return he wrote a book titled *Orthodoxy in the Holy Land*. "I found the Patriarchate [of Jerusalem] to be unattractive, ... care for the local Orthodox population is non-existent and its position is more dismal ... There is not one school, and it is better not to speak of the churches."[97] The Greek Church hierarchy was interested only in money and intrigues, in Khitrovo's words. Furthermore, while Orthodoxy was in decline spiritually and morally, the competitors of Orthodoxy, Protestantism and Catholicism, were increasing by leaps and bounds at the expense of Orthodoxy. In 1840, the Orthodox Christians numbered 90 percent of the Christians of Palestine, by 1880, their percentage had dropped to 67 percent. The decline was also perceptible in education. While the Catholics and the Protestants combined had about 82 schools, the Orthodox had only 2. Khitrovo told us that the decline of Orthodoxy resulted from the decline of the Greek clergy morally and spiritually.[98]

In 1881, the Russian Grand Duke Sergei Alexandrovich and his brother Paul paid a ten-day visit to the Holy Land. Khitrovo had already sent Sergei a copy of his book *Orthodoxy in the Holy Land* in which Khitrovo discussed the status of Orthodoxy and Russia's interests in Syria-Palestine. In February of the following year, Khitrovo and Duke Sergei met to discuss Khitrovo's ideas and the Society he was organizing. Both men agreed that a society was needed and Khitrovo agreed to draft the Society's constitution. When the constitution was ready, a copy was sent to the new Tsar Alexander III (r.1881–1894). The new tsar approved the constitution and the Society became a fact in St Petersburg in May 1882. Sergei accepted to serve as president. Khitrovo did not hold an official position in the Society until 1884, and at the urging of Sergei, he agreed to join the Society's council, and in 1889 he became the Society's secretary, a position he held until his death in 1903.[99]

What were the objectives of the Russian Orthodox Palestine Society? The Society was founded to address the worsening situation of Orthodoxy in Greater Syria, especially in Palestine. The Orthodox Arabs were suffering from spiritual and educational neglect and their Greek shepherds were doing nothing about it. Catholic and Protestant missionaries were preying on the Orthodox, encouraging them to convert to their Christian sects. The first objective of the Russian-Palestine Society was to collect, elaborate, and disseminate in Russia valid news about the holy places and the people of Palestine. Secondly, to render assistance to the Russian Orthodox pilgrims who came annually to visit the Holy Land and make their stay as comfortable as possible. Thirdly, to establish schools, hospitals, and hostels, and render material aid to native citizens, churches, monasteries, and clergy.[100] "An urgent need was the building of schools and churches in Palestine and support for the native Orthodox clergy.... Lack of Orthodox churches was causing the natives to lose their Orthodox consciousness. Lack of Orthodox schools was forcing parents to send their children to Catholic or Protestant institutions."[101] As the Society started to translate its objectives into concrete actions by restoring old churches and building new ones in the Jerusalem patriarchate, it was met with stubborn opposition and resistance from the Greek patriarch of Jerusalem and the Brotherhood of the Church of the Holy Sepulchre. (The Brotherhood of the Church of the Holy Sepulchre was established early in the sixteenth century. Membership was predominantly Greek. In time the Brotherhood came to dominate the patriarchate of Jerusalem spiritually and economically.) The patriarchate wanted to get hold of the funds and it would do the renovations. The society agreed until it found out that nothing was being done and the situation on the ground was getting worse rather than better.[102] The Society then decided to reorient its attention to education rather than renovating and restoring old churches. Also, to avoid more opposition in Jerusalem, the Society made the town of Nazareth its headquarters and the base of its operations. The Greek bishop of Nazareth was more friendly to the Society than the patriarch of Jerusalem. In 1889, the Jerusalem Patriarch Nikodemos resigned, and was replaced by Gerasimos, a former patriarch of Antioch, who continued hostility to the Society and its work. Because of this implacable hostility and obstruction, the Society decided to reduce its presence in Jerusalem and make Nazareth its headquarters. Additionally, from 1895 onward, the Society expanded its educational activity beyond Galilee to include the patriarchate of Antioch. Spiridon, patriarch of Antioch, welcomed the Society into his patriarchate, and so did the metropolitans of Tyre, Sidon (Saida), Beirut, Tripoli, and Homs.[103] School building began in Mujaidil, a center of foreign missionary activity in Galilee in 1883. This was the first society school. From Mujaidil, it spread to many villages, towns, and cities in Greater Syria.

If the residents of a town or village desired a Russian school, the residents built the school offering labor or money. Everything else was the responsibility of the Society: food, books, papers, pencils, ink, even clothing was given free of charge. Some schools already in operation were adopted by the Society. Some sources put the number of Russian schools built at 102 or 114 by the time World War I began in 1914.

Russian schools were basically primary schools except for two: Dar al-Mu'allimin, the Russian teacher training college in Nazareth for men, and its equivalent, Dar al-Mu'allimat, in Bait Jala for women. The last two were intended to provide teacher training to graduates of primary schools in order to qualify for teaching careers in primary society schools.

Although the Society reduced its activity in Jerusalem due to the opposition of the Greek clergy, it continued to buy land, build Russian churches in Jerusalem, fund archaeological research, and subsidize scholarly research in its methodological study of Palestine. The society came to control, or partly control, a Russian complex containing about 32 acres of land with buildings, churches, hostels, and hospitals. In 1889, the tsar approved the absorption of the former Palestine Committee by the Society and added the word "Imperial" to its name.[104]

Despite obstruction by the Greek clerical hierarchy, the Society remained true to its objectives. By the end of the nineteenth and beginning of the twentieth centuries, the Society was administering 67 schools in Palestine, with some 10,000 students and 45 schools in Syria. The society hospitals and clinics in Jerusalem, Bethlehem, Bait Jala, Nazareth, and Damascus admitted and treated approximately 100,000 patients. In 1901, 29,279 pilgrims visited the Holy Land. In January 1902, the value of the property owned by the Society amounted to 1,763,994 rubles.[105]

So, in an atmosphere of jubilation and triumph, the Imperial Orthodox Palestine Society celebrated its Silver Jubilee in May 1907 at Peterhof Palace in its founding city of St Petersburg (May 1882). The Imperial family, members of the Russian Holy Synod, high clergy, and administrators of the Society were in attendance. Meetings and church services were held. After twenty-five years of hard work, the Society was in possession of "2 million rubles worth of property, eight hostels for 10,000 pilgrims,"[106] in addition to the publication of some 347 books on the topic of Palestine and the holy places. While the Society was celebrating its Silver Jubilee, it was still administering over 100 schools with over 11,341 male and female students. "At the outbreak of the war [WWI], Russian influence was at its highest in Greater Syria. Besides four Russian churches in Jerusalem, there were many buildings ranging from hostels to hospitals, dispensaries and schools. In all parts of Syria and Palestine, one encountered evidence of the work of the Palestine Society. All this activity, however nonpolitical, increased Russian prestige in the area."[107]

Russian Schools vs Other Missionary Schools

There were significant differences between Russian schools and other missionary schools in Greater Syria. To begin with, Russian schools were totally free of charge. Tuition, room, and board were free. In addition, books, pens, pencils, paper, and notebooks were distributed to students free of charge.[108] Clothing and even pocket money, 6 rubles per student per month, were given at no charge to students or parents. No schools in the area treated their students the way the Society treated its students. Society students got comprehensive attention including free medical care. Worthy graduates of the Russian teacher training college in Nazareth were sent to study in Russia at the expense of the Society, including the well-known Mikha'il Nu'aimah of Baskinta, Lebanon.

Another characteristic of Russian schools was the fact that they were coeducational except in very few cases when boys and girls studied separately. Female education was not popular in Syria (and across the Middle East before World War I); only boys got some education. Russians didn't discriminate between the sexes. They admitted as many girls as boys, and in some cases girls were equal or outnumbered boys in some classes. Russian schools enhanced female education in Greater Syria. Hence, the female teacher training college in Bait Jala was as reputable as the Nazareth one for boys.

An important difference between Russian schools and others in the area was the quality of teaching. Russian schools had a higher quality. Whereas some traditional schools still depended on rote learning and physical punishment, Russian education emphasized teacher explanation of subject matter, analysis, and comprehension on the part of the student. Russian schools tried to cultivate the student's personality through respect and special attention, if needed. Physical punishment was prohibited. If a teacher happened to hit a student, the teacher was punished.

A very important difference between Russian schools and other French, American, or English schools was the fact that Russian schools were not truly missionary. The Russians did not come to Syria to convert the Muslims, Jews, Maronites, or Roman Catholics to Orthodoxy. In fact, the Russians were the last to enter Syria. The Russians came to Syria to defend Orthodoxy against the inroads that Catholicism and Protestantism were making into Orthodox towns and villages. Russian schools provided the Orthodox of Syria with an alternative education to French, American, or English education, and they succeeded. Russian schools accepted both Orthodox and non-Orthodox. They did not try to convert the non-Orthodox as the French, American, and English did. In fact, Russian education in Syria strengthened secularism. Although Russian schools offered courses on Orthodoxy, religion was not a strong topic.

Another important difference between Russian schools and other missionary schools was the fact that Russian schools emphasized teaching the Arabic language, whereas other missionary schools did not. Arabic was the language of instruction in Russian schools; it was the most important language. Although Russian schools taught Russian, the Russian language ranked third after Arabic. It wasn't emphasized. The Nazareth teacher training college was the first academic institution to offer Arabic literature. The Syrian Protestant College made Arabic the language of instruction first, then shifted to English. In French schools, French was the main language of instruction. Arabic was not emphasized. Similarly, in English schools, English was the main language of instruction. Unlike the French and English, the Russians emphasized Arabic from the very beginning as the national language of the Arabs. The fact that Russian schools emphasized the teaching of Arabic language and literature, this became an important factor in the revival of the Arabic language and Arab identity. Sati al-Husri, a modern Syrian writer, considered the revival of Arabic in Russian society schools as an important factor in the rise of Arab nationalism.

Nu'aimah, a graduate of the Nazareth Russian teacher training college , recognizes the influence of his Arabic Professor, Antoun Ballan, when he says, "what is more important, Professor Antoun was the first to awaken in us national feeling. He used to speak to us occasionally about the misery which our country has suffered from under the Turkish yoke, and about the absolutism of Sultan Abdul Hamid II and his crimes, and about the corruption which has spread in all the departments of the state starting with the sultan at the top and ending with the last mayor in the last village. It is imperative on the Arabs, if they want to be independent and live in honor and dignity to recover the usurped Caliphate from the Turks. The Caliphate belongs to the Arabs, and it is impermissible to transfer it to the Turks or Persians."[109]

Mikha'il Nu'aimah also spoke with nostalgia about his Russian school in Baskinta, the town of his birth. He relates that the Orthodox community of Baskinta got excited at the news that Russia had decided to build them a school. Some villagers volunteered money toward building the school; others volunteered labor. The school was built in 1899 and became operative rather immediately. "For the first time in its history Baskinta had what could be called an exemplary school. And for the first time in its history, Baskinta's daughters and sons went to school together. The school had five male teachers and three female ones, headed by a director who was a graduate of the Russian Nazareth teacher training college where he studied the art of education, teaching, and school administration. And for the first time we felt that we were at a school which had a curriculum and an academic calendar."[110] This was the school in which Nu'aimah had spent five years and the "school which influenced me the most and directed me all my life!"[111]

The Society's Structure

As stated previously, the Imperial Orthodox Palestine Society was established in St Petersburg on May 22, 1882. There were 43 founding members, 13 of whom belonged to the Imperial family. The tsar was the honorary president. Grand Duke Sergei served as president of the Society and Vasili Khitrovo served first as a council member and then as secretary of the Society. Sergei and Khitrovo were the midwives of the Society and guided it to maturity.

The Society had three categories of membership: honorary, regular, and supportive. Honorary membership was given to members of the imperial family or those who gave the Society a one-time gift of 5,000 rubles or more. Regular membership cost 25 rubles annually, or a one-time payment of 500 rubles for life. Honorary and regular memberships were limited but expanded through time. Supportive membership cost 10 rubles annually or a one-time payment of 200 rubles for life.[112] Membership in the Society increased slowly. To spread news about the society in Russia about 43 centers were established in major cities throughout Russia. By 1908, honorary members numbered 138, regular 887, and supportive 2,589.[113] Anybody could join the Society provided he/she agreed with its objectives, and fulfilled the terms of membership.

The Society's Budget

The society spent 350,000 rubles annually: 150,000 were allocated to pilgrims, 150,000 allocated to schools and churches, and 50,000 allocated to publications. The society got its income from membership dues, gifts, donations, church collections, income from real estate, and interest. In May 1900, the tsar agreed to grant the Society annually a gift of 30,000 rubles. Church collections on Palm Sunday all over Russia were earmarked for the Society. This was probably the Society's most important source of income.[114]

The finances of the Society were not stable. Income fluctuated from year to year. However, up until the end of the nineteenth century, the Society appeared to be doing well financially. Appearances, however, are sometimes deceiving. The twentieth century opened with the Russo-Japanese War of 1904–1905, in which Russia was badly defeated. As a result, the income of the Society decreased and never recovered, as the Society moved from one disaster to another.

At this point, and after about twenty-five years of its existence, it is important to raise the question of whether the Imperial Orthodox Palestine Society was faithful to the objectives which led to its birth. It will be recalled that Vasili Nikolaevich Khitrovo paid several visits to the Holy Land, the first of which was in 1871, and the second and third in 1880–1881 in which he stayed nine months. During these visits he studied, traveled, and observed a lot about what kind of relations existed between the Greek religious hierarchy and their Arab Orthodox flock in the Patriarchates of Jerusalem and Antioch. He also observed what Russian pilgrims went through in their pilgrimages to the holy places. The result of his experiences and observations was his book *Orthodoxy in the Holy Land* and the rise of the Orthodox Palestine Society in May 1882. The Society also was very close to the Imperial dynasty since the tsar was the honorary president and several Romanovs became members of the Society.

Did the Society improve the Pilgrims' lives while in Palestine? The answer is definitely in the affirmative. The Society had guides ready to lead the pilgrims as soon as they debarked at Jaffa, Jerusalem's port of entry. They walked from one place to another. The Society also built about eight hostels to accommodate about 10,000 pilgrims at the same time. The Society also built a hospital in Jerusalem and six clinics in different towns and cities to fulfill the pilgrims' medical needs. Room, board, and medical care were free of charge. Sometimes, pilgrims came for Christmas and lingered around for Easter. The Society also built four Russian cathedrals in Jerusalem to address the pilgrims' spiritual needs.

Did the Society improve the quality of life for the native Orthodox population of Greater Syria? Here again the answer is positive. The Society built new churches and renovated older ones. New icons and church utensils came from Russia. People started to go to church again. The Society's most important achievements, however, were in the area of education. Let us not forget that the Ottoman *millet* system made spiritual leaders responsible for the education of their *millet* members. The Greek religious hierarchy neglected this area totally. Vasili Khitrovo could not find one Orthodox school open! When the Society began to build schools to educate the Orthodox youth, the Greek clerical hierarchy resorted to all types of resistance and obstruction. It seemed like the Greeks did not want the Arabs to get educated, fearing Arab competition over top positions in the Church. Facing Greek hostility in Jerusalem, the Society relocated its headquarters to Nazareth and expanded the scope of its operations to the Patriarchate of Antioch where the Society was welcomed. From its new location, the Society initiated a program of school building in towns and villages across Greater Syria where education was mostly needed. More than 100 schools were built in places where Orthodox concentrations were found. If a village or town desired a Russian school, the villagers or town people built the school, offering money or labor. Once the school was built everything else became the responsibility of the Society: furniture, room and board, books, pencils, paper, even clothing.

Almost all Russian schools were primary schools except for two: the Nazareth teacher training college for boys (Dar al-Mu'allimin), and its equivalent in Bait Jala (Dar al-Mu'allimat) for girls. Graduates of primary schools enrolled in these two teacher training colleges in order to prepare them to fill teaching positions in the Society's primary schools. Promising graduates of the Russian Nazareth teacher training college were sent to Russia for graduate work. About nine students were sent to Russia to study at the expense of the Society, including the aforementioned Mikha'il Nu'aimah from Baskinta, Lebanon. Russian schools were very popular and competed strongly with Catholic, Protestant, and native schools. The two training schools at Nazareth and Bait Jala "were in some respects superior to existing institutions, and the Society was never able to satisfy the actual demand."[115]

The Russians helped keep the native Orthodox in their faith and strengthened the teaching of Arabic in their schools. Whereas French and Protestant schools were keen to "Westernize" their students, Russian schools stressed local food, dress, and traditions without aiming to "Russify" their students.[116]

At its establishment back in 1882, the Imperial Orthodox Palestine Society promised to make the Holy Land more familiar to the Russian people through research, writing, archaeological work, travel, and the pilgrimages. Here again the Society delivered on its promise. Within the span of about twenty-five years, Society scholars both Russian and non-Russian researched, examined, and published 347 books about Palestine and the holy places. The Society made a tremendous contribution to scholarship and the study of Palestine. "Never before did Russia witness such publication of primary and secondary sources on Palestine and the Christian East. Never before did the Russian people have such easy access to scholarly and popular accounts about the Holy Places."[117]

Enemies of the Society, Greek clerics, Catholics, Latins, Protestants, accused the Society of promoting Russian imperialism. The Society denied the accusation, but it continued. Greek clerics, although Orthodox, developed a grudge against the Society because it was building schools to educate Arab Orthodox youth in Greater Syria. This ran against the policy of the Greek clergy because they were against educating Arab Orthodox youth. "There is not one school open," Khitrovo said in his book. Catholics and Protestants were against the Society because it established a school system in Syria that successfully competed against theirs and proved superior to them. Students and parents who had renounced Orthodoxy and converted to Catholicism and Protestantism returned to Orthodoxy having found out that Russian schools were free and sound educationally. As a result, some missionary schools closed, others lost students especially in Nazareth. The British Consul confirmed that "apart from free supply of books, it was customary to give two free uniforms to every pupil in the year, so that for this or other reasons children in English missionary schools were lured to those of the Russians."[118] On the whole, it is a fact that a good number of successful teachers of Arabic and writers and journalists in Palestine in the first decades of the twentieth century received their education in Russian schools.[119]

Was the Imperial Orthodox Palestinian Society promoting Russian imperialism? A majority of writers I have consulted, Arab and non-Arab, reject the idea. Yūsuf al-Ḥakīm, a Syrian writer and a long-time Ottoman civil servant, says in his book on Syria that Russian schools in Latakia and all over Syria were never under suspicion because they limited themselves to the ideas of humanism and free education, not giving Orthodox Christians any reason to resort to

Western institutions, Latin or evangelical, which are rich in culture, wealth, and organization.[120] Theofanis G. Stavrou said that Russians did not try to Russify Syrians, and all schools were elementary except the two teacher training colleges of Nazareth and Bait Jala.[121] Constantin Basili, Russia's consul in Beirut (1839–1853), said that Russia's policy in Syria did not aspire to control Syria as the policies of Britain and France did. Russia did not have direct interest in Syria at the time.

Russia's interests lay farther north in the Black Sea and the Turkish Straits: free navigation.[122] The Russians came to Syria because of the historical relationships between the two Orthodox patriarchates of Antioch and Moscow. There was closeness and friendship for centuries, which have already been discussed. Furthermore, the Russians came to Syria to protect the Orthodox Christians of Syria against the incursions of Catholicism and Protestantism into Orthodox towns and villages. The Russians came to Syria to provide an alternative education to French and Protestant missionary education. The Russians came to Syria to defend a faith and not to introduce a new faith. Only one author, Agnes de Dreuzy, attributed political motivation to Russia in backing the Imperial Orthodox Palestine Society in its educational effort in Greater Syria. "Russia, the unofficial protector of the Greek Orthodox populations, was using the protectorate to put a foot in Palestine and eventually gain preeminence and political presence there."[123]

Needless to say, in this statement, the author made an assertion not backed by evidence.

Decline and Collapse

Russian schools in Syria suffered from some important weaknesses from the beginning. One weakness was lack of trained teachers, Arab and Russian. This was somewhat remedied by the establishment of the Nazareth and the Bait Jala teacher training colleges whose graduates filled teaching positions in the Society's primary schools across Greater Syria. The Society also had problems in recruiting qualified Russian teachers, male and female. Arabs also complained that some Russians appeared haughty and felt superior to them. Russian female teachers posed more of a problem. Agafangel Krymsky, a Russian writer who lived about two years in Beirut and Mount Lebanon, described some of them as "unfit to teach." Furthermore, they hated Beirut and its residents.[124] Krymsky explained their attitude as a result of isolating themselves and the lack of means of entertainment. They all left Beirut and the Society about the end of 1897.

Another serious problem the Society faced was the emigration of many of its graduates to Egypt, North America, and South America. Even some of the students who studied in Russia at the expense of the Society opted to stay in Russia or settle in North or South America. Society graduates also lacked the opportunity for higher education in Syria since Society schools were elementary except for the two teacher training colleges. Those students who wanted higher education had two alternatives: the Syrian Protestant College or St Joseph's Jesuit University in Beirut. Lastly, the society faced the problem of a progressively dwindling income, especially following the Russo-Japanese War of 1904–1905.

The opening of the twentieth century was extremely unkind to the Imperial Orthodox Palestine Society. It took away the two most important persons who founded the Society and steered it for about twenty-five years. Khitrovo, the secretary of the Society, passed on in 1903, and Grand Duke Sergei, the president, was assassinated two years later. They were the Society's captains from its foundation in 1882 until 1903–1905. They were two very capable men whose only mistake was probably not training others to take over after them.

With Sergei's death, his wife Grand Duchess Elizabeth Feodorovna (sister of Alexandra, wife of Tsar Nicholas II) became president of the Society, succeeding her husband. Under Elizabeth the decline of the Society accelerated as a consequence of the Russo-Japanese

War which was followed by the Russian Revolution of 1905. The Society's expenses went up while its income went down.

The Society's membership also decreased from 5,000 in 1904 to 3,000 in 1914. Church collections also decreased. In a nutshell, income could not keep up with expenses. The Russian government increased its annual contribution to 150,000 rubles annually, but this did not reverse the trend.

Meanwhile, the international situation in Europe was getting more complex and the European powers polarized into two opposing alliances: the Triple Entente of Britain, France, and Russia, and the triple Alliance of Germany, Austria-Hungary, and later, the Ottoman Empire. The incident that set the world aflame was the assassination of Francis Ferdinand, heir to the throne of Austria on June 28, 1914. The Ottoman Empire initially vacillated between neutrality and war, but international developments pushed it to join the war on Germany's side. As Turkey and Russia became enemies in World War I, Turkey confiscated all Russian property and closed Russian schools. Since Russia suffered heavily in the war in loss of life and devastation, this played into the hands of Vladimir Lenin, a socialist revolutionary who led the Bolshevik Revolution in Russia and seized power in October–November 1917. Tsar Nicholas II and his family were executed, followed by the second and last president of the Imperial Orthodox Palestine Society, Grand Duchess Elizabeth Feodorovna. After about thirty years of hard work and school building, the sun finally set on the Imperial Orthodox Palestinian Society, but its legacy survives.

The End of Greek Clerical Control of the Patriarchate of Antioch

By 1453 Constantinople, the capital of the Byzantine Empire, had become an island in an Ottoman Sea. The Ottomans had eaten up all its lands in Western Asia and East Europe, including Greece. Some

Ottoman sultans before Mehmet II (r. 1451–1481) tried to capture the city but failed. The city's defenses proved impregnable. When Mehmet II became sultan, his attention focused on Constantinople. The city at that time was completely a European city. He made elaborate preparations on land and sea in order to cut the city off from any potential support from Europe. Once he felt ready, he laid siege to the city in early April 1453, cutting it off from any communication by land or sea from Europe. The city's population was declining and there weren't enough men to defend the walls. At the same time Mehmet II used heavy artillery and gun powder against the city walls. April was approaching its end and Mehmet II was becoming desperate. He gathered his advisors for consultation. Some told him the city's defenses were strong and advised him to lift the siege. One advisor, Zagan Pasha, told the sultan that he noticed signs of weakness in the city's defenses and advised him to continue the siege. There was a Genovese contingent helping defend the city walls. Its commander was wounded and withdrew from the battle. His contingent followed him, creating more gaps in the city's defenses. In early May, Mehmet's artillery opened a gap in one of the walls and Muhammad's army poured in. The defenders were overwhelmed. Mehmet II allowed his army to pillage the city for three days. This was the army's payment. After three days, Mehmet restored law and order and opened the city for all—Jews, Muslims, and Christians to come and live in the city, renaming it as Istanbul and making it the capital of the Ottoman Empire. Having taken Constantinople, Mehmet took the title of "conqueror" and resumed the war against Central and Eastern Europe until his death in 1481.

Until the rise of Selim I (r. 1512–1520), no Ottoman sultan fought an Arab Muslim state. Sultan Selim I changed all of this. Claiming that the Sunni Mamluk State of Egypt and Syria was helping Shiite Iran against the Sunni Ottomans, he attacked Syria and defeated the Mamluks at Marj Dabiq near Aleppo in 1516. From Syria, Selim I occupied

Egypt and ended the Abbasid Arab Caliphate based in Cairo. Selim I assumed the title of caliph, the first non-Arab caliph, and the first Turkish caliph in Islam. The Turkish Caliphate lasted from 1517 to 1924.

With the acquisition of Greater Syria and Egypt, the Ottomans became rulers of millions of Christians, mostly Orthodox. The Ottomans followed the precedent set by Prophet Muhammad in dealing with the Christians and Jews of the Arabian Peninsula as he began to preach Islam starting in 610 A.D. In other words, Prophet Muhammad considered Jews and Christians as possessors of a divine message from Allah/God, the same God who revealed the Qur'an to him intermittently through the Angel Gabriel. Hence, Christians and Jews have been referred to as the "people of the book," people with holy religions revealed to them by Allah.

Christians and Jews were allowed to live autonomously in the Muslim state in accordance with their religions under their religious chiefs. This is what the Ottomans called the "millet system," *millet* meaning religious community. There were three *millets* in the Ottoman Empire: Muslim, Christian, and Jewish.

The *millet* system empowered religious leaders as heads of the *millets*. "The Greek Patriarch of Constantinople had been civil head of the Orthodox community of the Empire since 1453 . . . Gradually, the Greeks had extended their ecclesiastical control over the whole church: the Balkan patriarchates had been extinguished; the Patriarch of Antioch was normally Greek; those of Jerusalem and Alexandria were also Greek, ... while the revenues and government of the church in the Holy Land were in the hands of a tight, powerful, monastic brotherhood of the 'Holy Sepulchre' with a membership almost entirely Greek."[125]

"The majority of the Christians [in Palestine] belong to the Orthodox Greek Church, Arabic being the language generally spoken, though the superior clergy mostly come from the Greeks.

Although the church numbers at almost 51,000 souls, 7000 of whom live in Jerusalem, they are divided by this difference of language and nationality."[126]

"...in Syria the great majority of the laity and lower clergy were Arabic speaking. Even in the eighteenth century there were signs of discontent among them; this increased in the nineteenth, as the sense of ethnic and linguistic difference came to the surface of men's consciousness in the Near East, and still more because of the close connection of Russia with the Orthodox inside the empire..."[127]

It is obvious now that the Arab Orthodox Christians of Greater Syria were victims of two imperialisms simultaneously: a territorial imperialism by the Ottoman Turks, who controlled the land and everything on it, and spiritual imperialism by the Greek clerical hierarchy who monopolized top positions in the church and kept their flock, which they were supposed to take care of, ignorant, poor, and illiterate.

The second half of the nineteenth century, especially the last quarter, was a period of enlightenment and awakening politically and spiritually. Politically, some intellectuals and activists began to clamor and organize against Turkish domination and occupation which lasted about 400 years. They were inspired by a poem composed by Ibrahim Yaziji (1847–1906) in which he called upon the Arabs to rise up from their deep sleep and liberate the homeland from foreign occupation. Yaziji was one of the pioneers of the modern Arab literary renaissance. Spiritually, the movement to free the Orthodox Church of Greater Syria from Greek clerical domination gained momentum and support. Graduates of the Russian Teacher Training College of Nazareth led the movement in Palestine, in the Patriarchate of Jerusalem. As to the Patriarchate of Antioch, the movement came to a head in the early 1890s over the election of a new patriarch. Two parties crystallized: a Greek party composed of bishops, patriarchs, and pro-Greek laity who wanted to keep the status quo. This party had the support of the Greek government and the Ottoman government. The second party was the Arab Orthodox party composed of low-ranking Orthodox clergy and the majority of the people. They demanded an Arab patriarch. The Arab party had the sympathy of Russia which was against the domination of the Orthodox Church by the Greeks. When the Holy Synod met to elect a new patriarch for Antioch on October 2, 1891, it elected a Greek named Spiridon, a victory for the Greek party. The bishop of Beirut who favored the Arab party was barred from the meeting. The Orthodox Arabs rejected Spiridon as their patriarch, along with some other bishops, claiming that Spiridon's election was illegitimate. The Ottoman government recognized the election as legitimate. The late metropolitan of Tripoli, Elias Kurbān, claimed that Spiridon's election was the result of pressure, bribery, and unlawful interventions.[128] The Greek party accused Russia of direct intervention in the patriarchal election in the interest of the Arab party. Metropolitan Kurbān says that Russia was sympathetic to the Arab party but did not intervene directly the way Greece did. "There is no proof of direct Russian intervention in the election."[129]

Spiridon's Patriarchate lasted six tumultuous years. He was rejected as patriarch by the laity, along with three Arab bishops. Because the people rejected him, and because of a certain violation he committed, the Holy Synod deposed him, forcing his resignation on January 31, 1898.[130] With Spiridon's deposition and his eventual resignation, the position of patriarch was declared vacant, and a campaign soon started to elect a successor. There was an attempt to repeat the game which was played six years earlier. The Greek party wanted a Greek patriarch and was backed by the ecumenical patriarch of Constantinople, and the patriarchs of Jerusalem and Alexandria, all Greeks. The Ottoman government still backed the Greek party and wanted candidates from beyond the see of Antioch to nominate themselves and participate in the election. It didn't work. When the Holy Synod met on May 12, 1898, it elected Arab Meletius II Doumani, the Arab bishop of Latakia, to head the Patriarchate of Antioch: the first Arab patriarch in centuries.[131] After some delay and hesitation, the Ottoman government changed its position and recognized the new patriarch as legitimate. A similar movement was underway to Arabize the Patriarchate of Jerusalem. It failed, and the Greeks are still in control there. Derek Hopwood attributes the success of the Arabs in Antioch to the strong support they got from the Imperial Orthodox Palestine Society and Russia.[132] Albert Hourani, on the other hand, claims that "Arab nationalism began with the struggle of the Arab Orthodox to throw off Greek control in the Patriarchate of Antioch."[133]

Following the end of World War II and one year before his death, Joseph Stalin revived Russia's interest in the Near East with a focus on culture. Thus the old Imperial Orthodox Palestine Society was revived as the Soviet Palestine Society in 1952, and laid claim to the property which the former Tsarist Society had owned.

With the fall of Communism in 1989–1991, the Council of the Russian Federation decided in May 1992 that the Society should resume its activity under the old name. In Lebanon, a branch of the Society was established as a result of the initiative taken by some Russian Orientalists and local Lebanese, with the hope that the older Society would return as a scientific charitable society dedicated to human development in the Middle East. When Vladimir Putin visited Israel-Palestine in the latter part of May 2012, he commemorated the establishment of the Imperial Orthodox Palestine Society which was founded in May 1882. Putin has succeeded in recovering Russian ownership of some of the property that the Tsarist Society had owned in Palestine, including in Jerusalem.

Chapter 6

The Impact of the Imperial Orthodox Palestine Society

Despite its short life, barely thirty years, the Imperial Orthodox Palestine Society left considerable impact on Greater Syria, Palestine in particular. Between 1882 and 1895, the Society focused on Palestine. It made the city of Nazareth in Galilee, north Palestine, its base because of the opposition of the Greek Patriarchate in Jerusalem. After 1895, the Society expanded its activity to all parts of Greater Syria. All in all, the Society built about 114 schools between 1882 and 1914, 48 of them were in Lebanon, with 5 in Beirut. Schools were built in places where an Orthodox community was already established. Society schools were open to all denominations, with no discrimination or preference for Orthodox over non-Orthodox. All students were welcome. Whenever the Society decided to build a school in a town or village, the residents would build the physical structure and the Society would provide everything else. People would volunteer money or labor.

Russian schools were basically primary because this was what the people needed. Russian education was geared toward the mass of the people, not the upper classes. Only the two Teacher Training Colleges at Nazareth and Bait Jala were above primary level because they were intended to prepare graduates of primary schools to qualify as teachers in the Society's primary schools. The colleges were on high school level or a little higher.

Russian schools were tough; they had higher educational standards than Catholic, Protestant, or native schools. Teachers were required to analyze and explain the subject matter; students were supposed to comprehend it, not commit it to memory and recite it like a parrot—no rote learning. Arabic was the medium of education in Russian schools, taking priority over all others, including Russian, which occupied third place after Arabic and Math. Graduates of French missionary schools were strong in the French language, culture, and history, but weak in Arabic grammar, language, and history. Agafangel E. Krimsky the Russian scholar who lived in Beirut and Mount Lebanon for about two years toward the end of the nineteenth century describes the Beiruti's saying, "the Arabic residents of Beirut, with the exception of the older ones, wear European style clothing. But their elegant European appearance is only superficial. Many of them, or rather most of them, chatter in French. A Jesuit student told me that. It is amazing how strong French influence is here. People think if they know French, that is all there is to know."[134]

As already stated, unlike English and French missionary schools, Russian ones emphasized the Arabic language, Arabic grammar and written Arabic, plus the study of the history of Arabic literature. Mikha'il Nu'aimah confirmed that the Russian Teacher Training College of Nazareth was unique in the fact that it was the first academic institution which included in its curriculum the study of Arabic literature and its history.[135] Nu'aimah graduated from the primary Russian school of Baskinta whose director was a graduate of the Russian Teacher Training College of Nazareth. He advised Nu'aimah to go to the Nazareth Teacher Training College to continue his studies there, which Nu'aimah did.

Because of his outstanding performance and character, the Society sent him to Russia for higher education. Similarly, Alexander Kuzma of Damascus graduated from the Russian Teacher Training College and was sent to Russia for graduate work. Following his graduation, he was chosen to head the Russian college at Nazareth and remained in his position until 1914. As director of the Russian Teacher Training College, Kuzma insisted that students in Russian schools must wear Arab dress, not European. Teaching the Arabic language, history, and literature and wearing Arabic dress contributed to the rise of national awareness, national identity, and ultimately, Arab nationalism.

Graduates of the Russian Teacher Training College of Nazareth were in the forefront of those who fought for the Arabization of the Orthodox Patriarchates of Jerusalem and Antioch, calling for an end to Greek control. This was an important contribution of Russian schools to Arabism.[136]

Graduates of the Russian Nazareth Teacher Training College and those of its equivalent in Bait Jala filled numerous teaching positions not only in the towns and villages of Palestine, but also in Syria and Lebanon as well. In this sense, graduates of Russian schools manifested the unity of Greater Syria at its best. It didn't make any difference where you came from, Lebanon, Syria, or Palestine. Russian school graduates also filled teaching and administrative positions throughout the duration of the British mandate in Palestine, 1920–1948.[137] In celebrating the Society's Silver Jubilee in 1907, Alexander Kuzma told the audience that 170 students enrolled in the Nazareth College from its foundation until September 1906. Of the 170 students, 50 were still studying, 58 have graduated and filled teaching positions in the Society's schools—54 from Palestine and 4 from Syria; 9 students were sent to Russia for graduate work at the expense of the society.[138]

Some Nazareth College graduates tried to make their mark in literary prose, verse, novels, and short stories. They were more productive in prose rather than verse. Some became translators of Russian literature into Arabic. Before the 1890s, the Arabs were little familiar with Russian literature. As more students learned Russian in Russian schools, they began to translate from Russian to Arabic. Hence, graduates of Russian schools introduced Russian literature to Arab readers and some fell in love with it. Mikha'il Nu'aimah became exposed to Russian literature at the Nazareth Russian Teacher Training College and more so when he went to study in Russia. In his own words, it changed his life. He found Russian literature was full of life, whereas Arab literature in comparison was lifeless. He became part of a movement which called for more liberalism, reform, and renewal in Arab literature (*Tajdīd*).

Other graduates of the Russian Teacher Training College of Nazareth became journalists or editors of magazines and papers wherever they settled in Palestine, Egypt, and North and South America. Half the members of the Pen League (al-Rabita al-Qalamiyya)[139] of New York and Boston were graduates of the Russian Teacher Training College.

They were activists for reform and social change. In their country of birth, they called for improvement in the status of women. Historically, Middle Eastern society was indifferent to women's education. Russian schools did not discriminate against women. Russian schools were mostly coeducational, with the number of girls almost equal or more than the number of boys. Graduates of Dar al-Mu'allimat of Bait Jala, like those of the Nazareth Teacher Training College, filled teaching positions in the Society's schools all over Syria. They called for renewal (*Tajdīd*) and reform both in society and in Arab literature.

As to Orthodoxy, Russian schools provided the Orthodox Christians of Greater Syria an alternative to Catholic and Protestant education. Before the appearance of Russian schools, and because of the lack of Orthodox schools, Orthodox students attended Catholic and Protestant schools and ended up converting to Catholicism and Protestantism in significant numbers. In the 1840s, Orthodox Christians made up 90 percent of the Christians of Syria. By about 1880, their percentage had diminished to 67 percent. Some observers predicted the disappearance of Orthodoxy in Syria within a century. Henry

Jessup, an American missionary who spent fifty-three years in Syria, commented saying, "I am almost amazed at the extent to which evangelical light pervades the nominally Christian communities here. The Greek Church in Beirut will go over some day to Protestantism *en masse* if the light continues to spread in the future as it has in the past ten years. A prominent Greek [Orthodox] said a few days ago, 'You Protestants need not trouble yourselves about converting Syria. Our children are all going to be Protestants whether you will or not. The Bible is doing the work.'"[140] This was the situation before the appearance of the Russians on the scene in 1882. With the appearance of the Russians on the Syrian stage, things began to change.

The Russians established a system of education that was totally free and surpassed those introduced by the Catholic and Protestant missionaries. There was no need for Orthodox students to attend non-Orthodox schools any longer. The Russians reversed the trend. Even those Orthodox families who had converted to Catholicism and Protestantism under missionary pressure and temptations returned to Orthodoxy. As a result, Catholic and Protestant missionary schools lost students and some had to close.

A lasting contribution of the Imperial Orthodox Palestine Society is the Society's scholarly contribution preserved in some 347 books researched and published by the Society's scholars, architects, archaeologists, historians, etc. This scholarly contribution escaped the destruction and devastation of the Bolshevik Revolution of October–November of 1917, and may still be available to interested researchers.

The Society's legacy is still alive. It is carved in cathedral stones in Jerusalem, Nazareth and school buildings all over Greater Syria. Some Lebanese, Syrians, and particularly Palestinians still remember Russian schools[141] with nostalgia and thankfulness as Mikha'il Nu'aimah did to the end of his life. It is amazing that so much was done in such a short time.

APPENDIX: Missionary Activity and Imperialism

Unfortunately, the negative implications of European imperialism, abuse, exploitation, oppression, and sometimes death were not limited to the natives of the Old World only. In the Western Hemisphere, the attempt by the Spanish, British, and French missionaries to Christianize and Westernize Native Americans with the help of local political authorities has factored in the death of thousands of them.

Several articles published by the *New York Times* recently (2021–2022) documented the agony, suffering, and even death of numerous young Native Americans in the United States and Canada in an attempt to acculturate them and make them live like white Europeans, French or English.[142]

Special boarding schools were built in British Colombia and Saskatchewan in Canada, and Colorado, Arizona, California, and Nebraska in the United States. This "experiment" lasted more than 113 years in the former and some 150 years in the latter. Young children, boys and girls, were forcibly removed from their families and tribal environment and forced to live in these boarding schools, totally severed from their past. As soon as they arrived at these schools, their old clothes were taken away from them and they were given Western style clothing. Their heads were shaved, they could not eat their traditional food, speak their tribal language, or worship their own tribal gods. They were converted to Christianity, becoming either Catholic or Protestant, depending on the sect of the school they attended. However, despite differences in religious sects, the experiences of these young boys and girls, whether in the United States or Canada, were strikingly similar. "We couldn't eat our food, speak our language, and we couldn't sing our prayer songs." The net result of this experiment was not only "cultural genocide," but also physical genocide as well. These young boys and girls were abused physically, sexually, and emotionally. Violence and physical punishment were rampant. Many children died, some were killed and some just "disappeared." Many small graves were found both in the United States and Canada. Estimates of the dead in Canada range between 10,000 and 50,000, perhaps more.

In the opening of January 2022, the Canadian government pledged $31.5 billion dollars ($40 million Canadian), to settle its conflict with indigenous Canadian tribes and address the conditions which produced it.[143] Half the money would be used to compensate families who unwillingly gave up their children to those special boarding schools never to see them again. The other half would go to reform the educational system which produced the residential schools.

Sadly, the Catholic Church was a contributor to this human tragedy. Its role was to run those Catholic schools for the government. So did Protestant denominations. In March 2022, Pope Francis received a delegation representing two major native Canadian indigenous tribes. The delegation was seeking a formal papal apology for the involvement of the Catholic Church in running those schools for more than a century. The pope appeared sympathetic to the delegation's objective and expressed his sorrow for the abuse the children had suffered, but issued no formal apology then. Instead, he intimated that he might visit Canada sometime in the near future and would address the issue there. On the whole, the delegation seemed satisfied with the Pope's response.

Pope Francis kept his word. In the last week of July, 2022, he made a six day visit to Canada where he officially apologized to the indigenous people in their own habitat for the abuses committed by the Catholic Church while running the residential schools for the government, numbering about 130 schools, starting in the 1870s and lasting until about 1996. "I humbly beg forgiveness for the evil committed by Christians against the indigenous peoples," the pope said to a large crowd made up of mostly native Canadians. He also visited a cemetery where many young people were buried in unmarked graves. Looking tired, sickly and in a wheelchair, the pope said, "I am sorry, I ask forgiveness, in particular for the ways in which members of the church and religious communities cooperated, not least through their indifference, in projects of cultural destruction and forced assimilations promoted by the governments of the time which culminated in the system of residential schools." The pope also expressed his sorrow "for the ways in which many Christians supported the colonizing mentality of the powers that oppressed the indigenous peoples."[144] The pope seemed truly moved by what he saw and experienced in Canada.

The reaction of the indigenous people was mixed. Some considered the Pope sincere and meant well. "He clearly understands the evil of colonization," a survivor of a residential school said. "I was touched by what I heard," he continued. Some were indifferent while a few were critical of the Catholic Church because the church had promised to pay survivors of indigenous schools $25 million Canadian dollars in compensation. It only paid $1.2 million.

Fig 1 Antiochian Patriarch Macarius III al-Za'im visited Moscow in the 1650s and in 1666.

Fig 2 Metropolitan Philaret of Moscow (1782–1867) was a strong supporter of Orthodoxy in Syria.

Fig 3 A chromolithograph of a photo taken in May 1887 of Russian pilgrims in the Holy Land visiting the oak of Mamre where Abraham and Sarah entertained three holy angels: the Holy Trinity. (Genesis 18)

Fig 4 Russian Orientalist Vasili Nikolaevich Khitrovo wrote *Orthodoxy in the Holy Land* after a pilgrimage in 1871 and drafted the first constitution of the Russian Orthodox Palestine Society.

Fig 5 Tsar Alexander III. He approved the constitution of the Russian Orthodox Palestine Society that was enacted in May 1882.

Fig 6 Lithograph depicting pilgrims visiting the Edicule surrounding the tomb of Christ: the Holy Sepulchre. A stamp on the card gives the date of 20 August 1881.

Fig 7 Grand Duke Sergei Alexandrovich the first president of the Russian Orthodox Palestine Society.

Fig 8 Grand Duchess Elizabeth Feodorovna succeeded her husband as president of the Society.

Fig 9 On pilgrimage in Jerusalem. At the consecration of the Church of St Mary Magdalen in Jerusalem in 1888. Right to left: Grand Duke Sergei Alexandrovich, Grand Duke Paul Alexandrovich, and the Grand Duchess Elizabeth, Lady E.N. Kozlianinova, and Archimandrite Antonin (Kapustin).

Fig 10 The "Russian Zone" or Sergievskoe Compound in Jerusalem flying the Imperial Orthodox Palestine Society flag. (1889) The society came to control this complex containing various buildings, churches, hostels, and a hospital.

Fig 11 The tower of the compound in 2020.

Fig 12 In 1864 the Holy Trinity Cathedral was consecrated; having been built within the compound, it was surrounded by hostelries for pilgrims.

Fig 13 The Society built a hospital in Jerusalem and six clinics in different towns and cities to fulfill the pilgrims' medical needs. This photo shows the Municipal Hospital within the Russian compound in 1920.

Fig 14 The Russian Teacher Training College in Bait Jala in 1892. Many graduates taught in the Society's primary schools.

Fig 15 Mikha'il Nu'aimah — poet, novelist, and member of the Pen League— was a graduate of the training college in Nazareth. (His English pen name is Mikhail Naimy.) He is pictured here with Pen League members Nasib 'Arida, Kahlil Gibran, and Abd al-Masih Haddad.

Fig 16 The Antiochian Patriarch Gregory IV (Haddad) who presided over the liturgical celebrations 300 years of Romanov rule in 1913.

ACKNOWLEDGMENTS

First I would like to thank the Very Reverend Thomas Zain of the Antiochian Orthodox Christian Archdiocese of New York and all North America for reading the manuscript and making valuable comments on it. He has my deepest appreciation.

Special thanks go to the staff of the Jafet Library of the American University of Beirut, Lebanon, where I did most of the research toward this book. They were cooperative and helpful in locating books, magazines, and paper articles relevant to my research.

Also, special thanks go to my niece Jacqueline E. Abodeely for typing the manuscript.

Her patience is unlimited. I cannot thank her enough.

Lastly, I want to thank Miss Mary Flibbert, Secretary of the History Department at Worcester State University for putting the final touches to the manuscript. Mary has a positive attitude and does her work with unmatched expertise and professionalism. Thank you Mary.

Najib E. Saliba

NOTES

Chapter 1

1. *Encyclopedia Americana*, Vol. 24 (USA, 1983), p. 27; ibid., Vol. 28, pp. 196–197.
2. Ibid., Vol. 15, p. 617.
3. *al-Kalima* (*the Word*), Vol. I (1905), pp. 73–75 (in Arabic); Balamand University, *Russia and the Orthodox of the East*, Balamand University, 1998 (in Arabic), pp. 65–66, 153–154, 202; Robert Haddad, *Syrian Christians in Muslim Society* (Princeton University Press, Princeton, 1970), pp. 83–84.
4. *Encyclopedia Americana*, Vol. 24, p. 27b; *Russia and the Orthodox of the East*, pp. 65, 235.
5. *Encyclopedia Americana*, Vol. 20, p. 348; *al-Kalima*, 1905, pp. 73–74.
6. *al-Kalima*, 1905, pp. 73–74.
7. Ibid., 1912, pp. 65, 66, Asad Rustum, *History of the Church of Antioch*, III, 1453–1928, Beirut, n.d., p. 191.
8. Rustum, *History of the Church of Antioch*, III, p. 364; Yūsuf al-Ḥakīm, *Beirut and Lebanon under the Ottomans* (Beirut, 1966), p. 62.
9. *Russia and the Orthodox of the East*, p. 88.
10. Ibid., p. 88.
11. *al-Kalima*, 1913, pp. 280–296, p. 628.
12. Ibid., 1913, pp. 292–293; ibid., 1914, pp. 78–80; Yūsuf al-Ḥakīm, *Syria in the Ottoman Period* (Beirut, 1966), pp. 132–133.
13. Rustum, III, p. 370.

14. *al-Lliqa al-Orthothoksi* (*The Orthodox Encounter*) (Beirut, 2017), p. 104.
15. Metropolitan Elias Kurbān, *Memories* (*Kalimat wa-Dhikrayat*), (Lebanon, n.d.), p. 259 (in Arabic).
16. The whole message is found in Arabic in *Russia and the Orthodox of the East* (Balamand University Publication, 1998), pp. 11–13.

Chapter 2

17. Balamand University, *Russia and the Orthodox Christians of the East* (Lebanon, 1998), p. 234.
18. Ibid., Derek Hopwood, *The Russian Presence in Syria and Palestine, 1843–1914* (Clarendon Press, Oxford, 1969), p. 12.
19. *al-Lliqa al-Orthothoksi* (*The Orthodox Encounter*) (Beirut, 2017), pp. 119–120.
20. G.J.S. Eversley, *The Turkish Empire,* 1228–1924 (Howard Fertig, New York, 1969), p. 221.
21. Encyclopedia Americana (Vol. 16, 1983), p. 593; Theofanis G. Stavrou, *Russian Interests in Palestine, 1882–1914* (Institute for Balkan Studies, Thessaloniki, 1963), p. 21.
22. Albert Hourani, *Arabic Thought in the Liberal Age, 1789–1939* (Oxford University Press, London, 1967), p. 40; A.J. Baker, *The War against Russia* (Halt, Rinehart and Winston, New York, 1971) p. 7; Ḥannā Abū Ḥannā, *The Vanguards of the Renaissance in Palestine (Graduates of Russian Schools), 1862–1914,* Beirut, 2005, p. 21; Asad Rustum, *History of the Church of Antioch,* III, 1453–1928 (Beirut, n.d.), p. 164; Fu'ad Farah, *The Living Stones, Arab Christians in the Holy Land,* Nazareth, 2003 (in Arabic), pp. 232–233.
23. Mitchell B. Garrett and James L. Godfrey, *Europe since 1815* (Appleton-Century-Crofts, New York, 1947), pp. 247–252; Hopwood, p. 6.
24. Eversley, pp. 294–299.

Chapter 3

25. *Russia and the Orthodox of the East* (Balamand University, 1998), pp. 24, 95, 138–139, 202 (in Arabic).
26. *al-Lliqa al-Orthothoksi (The Orthodox Encounter)* (Beirut, 2017), p. 39 (in Arabic).
27. Ibid.
28. Ibid.
29. Asad Rustum, *History of the Church of Antioch*, III, 1453–1928 (Beirut, n.d.), p. 201.
30. Derek Hopwood, *The Russian Presence in Syria and Palestine, 1843–1914* (Clarendon Press, Oxford, 1969), p. 56.
31. *Russia and the Orthodox of the East*, p. 158; *The Orthodox Encounter*, pp. 45–46; Yūsuf al Hakim, *Syria in the Ottoman Period* (Beirut, 1966), p. 193 (in Arabic).
32. *Russia and the Orthodox of the East*, p. 118; Yūsuf Daghir, *al Madrasah al-Miskobiyyah (The Russian School)*, an Orthodox Christian publication #3, al Sa'ih bookstore, Tripoli, Lebanon, 1982, a reprint.
33. Mikha'il Nu'aimah, *Sab'un 1889–1959, The Story of My Lifetime* (Sadir Press, Beirut, 1959), p. 150.
34. The number of Pilgrims differ slightly from one source to another. However sources agree that the number went up steadily from the end of the 1850s up to the outbreak of World War I. *al- Mahabba* magazine lists some numbers for the 1890s as follows:

Year	Pilgrims	
1891	5882	
1895	3070	
1896	3001	
1898	3299	
1900	5204	*al-Mahabba*, December 31, 1901

D. Hopwood:

1883–84	2145	
1895–96	4852	
1899–1900	11,000	

T. Stavrou:

1888–89	3000	
1894	4000	
1895	4852	
1895–99	26,104	
1910	15,000	9,000 were Russians
1913	12,000	last pilgrimage before WWI

35. Hopwood, pp. 35–36; *Russia and the Orthodox of the East,* p. 241; Rustum, III, p. 202.
36. *Russia and the Orthodox Christians of the East,* p. 142.
37. Theofanis G. Stavrou, *Russian Interests in Palestine. 1882–1914* (Institute for Balkan Studies, Thesaloniki, 1963), p. 38; Hopwood, p. 37.
38. Hopwood, p. 36; Stavrou, p. 78; *Russia and the Orthodox of the East,* p. 118; A.L. Tibawi, *A Modern History of Syria* (St. Martin's, 1969), p. 172.
39. Stavrou, p. 43; Abd al-Rahman Yaghi, *Modern Palestinian Literature,* (publication and distribution center, Beirut, 1968), pp. 30–31.

Chapter 4

40. Ḥannā Abū Ḥannā, *The Vanguards of the Renaissance in Palestine: Graduates of Russian Schools,* 1862–1914 (Beirut, 2005), p. 16; A.L. Tibawi, *Modern History of Syria* (St Martin's, 1969), p. 105; A.L. Tibawi, *American Interests in Syria.* 1800–1901 (Clarendon Press, Oxford, 1966), p. 17.

41. Tibawi, *American Interests in Syria,* p. 118; George Antonius, *The Arab Awakening,* Khayats (Beirut, 1938), p. 35; Phillip Mansel, *Aleppo*: The Rise and Fall of Syria's Great Merchant City (I.B. Tauris, London, New York, 2018) p. 34; Antonius, pp. 44–45.
42. Derek Hopwood, *The Russian Presence in Syria and Palestine,* 1843–1914 (Clarendon Press, Oxford, 1969), pp. 31, 99–100.
43. Mas'ūd Ḍā hir, *Beirut and Mount Lebanon about 1900,* a Study in Social History Based on the Memoirs of the Russian Scholar Agafangel Krymsky, 1871–1942 (Dar al-Mada, Beirut, 1985), p. 111.
44. Tibawi, *American Interests in Syria,* p. 311.
45. Agnes de Dreuzy, *The Holy See and the Emergence of the Modern Middle East, Benedict XV's Diplomacy in Greater Syria, 1914–1922* (Catholic University Press, Washington, DC, n.d.), p. 225.
46. Ibid.
47. A.L. Tibawi, "The Genesis and Early History of the Syrian Protestant College," *Middle East Journal* [MEJ], 21:1 (w.1967), Part I, pp. 1–15, p. 2; Antonius, p. 36.
48. Tibawi, *American Interests in Syria,* p. 33.
49. Ibid., p. 42.
50. Tibawi, "Genesis," Part I, p. 8.
51. Ibid.
52. Ibid., p. 99.
53. Usāma Makdisī, *Artillery of Heaven* (Cornell University Press, 2008), p. 190.
54. Gregory M. Wartabet, *Syria and the Syrians,* Vol. I (London, 1856), p. 270; Asad Rustum, *History of the Church of Antioch,* III, 1453–1928 (Beirut, n.d.), pp. 192–193.
55. Tibawi, *American Interests in Syria,* pp. 120–121.
56. Ibid., p. 143.
57. Tibawi, *A Modern History of Syria,* p. 114.
58. Tibawi, *American Interests in Syria,* pp. 35–36.

59. Ibid., pp. 150–152.
60. Ibid., p. 153.
61. Tibawi, "Genesis," Part I, p. 5.
62. Wartabet, *Syria and the Syrians*, p. 49.
63. Tibawi, *American Interests in Syria*, p. 39.
64. Ibid., p. 163.
65. Ibid., p. 79.
66. A district of southern Lebanon.
67. Tibawi, *A Modern History of Syria*, p. 106.
68. Robert Haddad, *Syrian Christians in Muslim Society* (Princeton University Press, Princeton, 1970), p. 80.
69. Ibid., p. 80 (quoting H.H. Jessup, *The Greek Church and Protestant Missions* (New York, 1891), pp. 6, 18, 22) [Orthodox Christians in Greater Syria are called "Greek Orthodox."].
70. Tibawi, *American Interests in Syria*, p. 282.
71. Tibawi, "Genesis," Part II, *MEJ*, 21:2 (1967), pp. 208–209.
72. Quoted by Abū Ḥannā, *The Vanguards*, pp. 50–51.
73. Yūsuf A. Daghir, *al-Madrasah al-Moskobiyya*, III (The Russian School), p. 5.
74. Masʿūd Ḍā hir, *Beirut and Mount Lebanon*, pp. 262–263.
75. Balamand University, *Russia and the Orthodox of the East* (Balamand, 1998), pp. 126–127 (in Arabic).
76. Ḍā hir, p. 39 (quoting Krymsky); Hopwood, pp. 30–31, 57, 99–100; Nicola Ziadeh, *Christianity and the Arabs* (Cadmos Press, Damascus, 2000), pp. 238, 254.
77. Tibawi, *American Interests in Syria*, p. 101.
78. Ibid., p. 118; Yūsuf al-Ḥakīm, *Syria under Faisal I* (The Catholic Press, Beirut, 1966), p. 99 (in Arabic).
79. To add insult to injury, China was forced to pay a large indemnity to compensate the victors, and granted them additional trade concessions which resulted in more foreign penetration of China.

80. Tibawi, *American Interests in Syria*, p. 4; George Stavrou Theofanis, *Russian Interests in Palestine*, 1882–1914 (Institute for Balkan Studies, Thessaloniki, 1963), p. 26.
81. Julius Richter, *A History of Protestant Missions in the Near East* (Edinburgh and London, 1910), p. 229.

Chapter 5

82. Najib Saliba, *The Province of Syria (Wilayat Suriyya) 1876–1909*, an unpublished doctoral dissertation (University of Michigan, 1971), pp. 317, 325; Joseph Zaytun, *al-Asiyyah*, 1840–1900 (an Orthodox patriarchal school in Damascus), an unpublished study in Arabic, pp. 21, 22–23.
83. A.L. Tibawi, *American Interests in Syria*, 1800–1901 (Clarendon Press, Oxford, 1966), p. 67.
84. Ibid.
85. Saliba, p. 330.
86. Ibid., p. 331.
87. Tibawi, *American Interests in Syria*, p. 118.
88. Constantin Pitkivich, *Lebanon and the Lebanese* (al-Mada Press, Beirut, 1986), p. 134.
89. Ibid., p. 151.
90. Tibawi, *American Interests in Syria*, p. 118.
91. George Antonius, *The Arab Awakening* (Khayats, Beirut, 1938), pp. 37–38.
92. Pitkivitch, p. 136.
93. Derek Hopwood, *The Russian Presence in Syria and Palestine*, 1843–1914 (Clarendon Press, Oxford, 1969), p. 30.
94. Tibawi, p. 118.
95. Robert Haddad, *Syrian Christians in Muslim Society* (Princeton University Press, Princeton, 1970), p. 61.
96. Pitkivich, p. 137; Ziadeh, Nicola, *Christianity and the Arabs* (Cadmus Press, Damascus, 2000), pp. 238, 254 (in Arabic).

97. Quoted by Hopwood, p. 101.
98. Theofanis G. Stavrou, *Russian Interests in Palestine*, 1882–1914 (Institute of Balkan Studies, Thessaloniki, 1963), p. 64.
99. Hopwood, p. 105.
100. Stavrou, p. 76; Mas'ūd Ḍā hir, *Beirut and Mount Lebanon about the Beginning of the 20th Century* (Dar al-Mada, Beirut, 1985), p. 153 (in Arabic); *al-Kalima* (1907), pp. 289–90; *al-Kalima* is the official Antiochian Orthodox publication in North America. It was in Arabic; now it is published in English.
101. Stavrou, p. 78.
102. Hopwood, pp. 114–115; Shukri K. Swaidan, *History of the Imperial Orthodox Palestinian Society* (Boston, 1912), pp. 154–155. Mr. Swaidan was a graduate of the Russian Seminar of Nazareth (the book is in Arabic).
103. Stavrou, p. 187; Yūsuf A. Daghir, *al-Madrasa al-Miskobiyya* [the Russian School], Tripoli, 1982 (in Arabic), p. 7; Hopwood, p. 113.
104. Hopwood, pp. 109–110, 114–15; Yūsuf al-Ḥakīm, *Syria in the Ottoman Period* (Beirut, 1966), pp. 193–94 (in Arabic).
105. *al-Mahabba*, June 15, 1902; pp. 343–344; *al-Manar*, November 1901, pp. 509–510.
106. Hopwood, p. 131 n.2; *al-Kalima*, 1907, p. 289; Swaidan, pp. 30–31, 84, 90.
107. Stavrou, p. 200.
108. Nu'aimah, *Sab 'un*, p. 142.
109. Ibid.; Ḥannā Abū Ḥannā, *The Russian Seminar in Nazareth*, 1886–1914 (Nazareth, 1994), p. 29.
110. Nu'aimah, *Sab'un*, p. 75, 142.
111. Ibid.
112. Stavrou, pp. 69–70, 80.
113. Swaidan, p. 200; Hopwood, p. 105.
114. Hopwood, p. 106; *al-Kalima*, 1907, p. 291.

115. A.L. Tibawi, "Russian Cultural Penetration of Syria and Palestine in the Nineteenth Century," *Journal of the Royal Central Asian Society*, 53:3, Part II, pp. 309–323, 314.
116. Ibid., p. 314.
117. Stavrou, p. 207.
118. Tibawi, "Russian Cultural Penetration," pp. 176–77.
119. Ibid.
120. Yūsuf al-Ḥakīm, *Syria in the Ottoman Period* (Beirut, 1966), p. 103 (in Arabic).
121. Stavrou, p. 166.
122. Constantin Basili, *Syria, Lebanon and Palestine under Turkish Rule* (Beirut, 1988), pp. 9–10 (in Arabic).
123. Agnes de Dreuzy, *The Holy See and the Emergence of Modern Middle East: Benedict XV's Diplomacy in Greater Syria*, (1914–22) (The Catholic University of America Press, Washington, DC, n.d.), p. 224.
124. Mas'ūd Ḍā hir, *Beirut and Mount Lebanon about the Beginning of the 20th Century*; a study in social history based on the memoir of the Russian Scholar Agafangel Krymsky (1871–1942), Dar al-Mada, Beirut, 1985 (A. Krymsky lived in Beirut and Mount Lebanon from 1896–1898.), pp. 36–37.
125. Albert Hourani, *Arabic Thought in the Liberal Age*, 1798–1939 (Oxford University Press, London, 1967), p. 273.
126. Julius Richter, *A History of Protestant Missions in the Near East* (Edinburgh and London, 1910), pp. 232–233.
127. Hourani, pp. 273–274.
128. Asad Rustum, *History of the Church of Antioch*, III, 1453–1928 (Beirut, n.d.), p. 254; Metropolitan Elias Kurbān, *The Crisis of the Antiochian Orthodox Patriarchate*, 1891–1899 (Tripoli, Lebanon, 1979), pp. 55–58.
129. Kurbān, p. 92.
130. Rustum, III, p. 268; Hopwood, p. 166.

131. Rustum, III, pp. 270–71; Kurbān, p. 121.
132. Hopwood, pp. 167–72.
133. Hourani, p. 315.

Chapter 6

134. Agafangel Krymsky, *Beirut and Mount Lebanon about the Beginning of the 20th Century* (1896–98) (Dar al-Mada, Beirut, 1985), p. 111. The book was translated into Arabic by Yūsuf ʻAtallah; Revised and corrected by Dr. Masʻūd Ḍā hir.
135. Ḥannā Abū Ḥannā, *The Russian Seminar of Nazareth,* 1886–1914 (Nazareth, 1994), pp. 126–128 (in Arabic).
136. A.L. Tibawi, "Russian Cultural Penetration of Syria and Palestine in the Nineteenth Century," Journal of the Royal Central Asian Society, 53:3, Part II, pp. 309–23, 321.
137. Abū Ḥannā, p. 36.
138. Ibid., pp. 24–25.
139. al-Rabitah al-Qalamiyya included well-known Arab literary figures like Gibran Khalil Gibran, Amin Rihani, Mikha'il Nu'aimah, and several others. They all belonged to the first wave of emigration from Greater Syria to the United States, which ended with the outbreak of World War I.
140. Henry H. Jessup, *Fifty-Three Years in Syria,* 2 Vol. (Fleming H. Revell Company, New York, 1910), Vol. I, p. 353.
141. Some Russian schools are preserved and open to visitors, such as Mikha'il Nu'aimah's school in Baskinta.

Appendix

142. Ian Austen, "At Canada's Native Schools a Grim Legacy of Cultural Erasure," NYT, July 6, 2021; Rukmini Callimachi, "Lost Lives, Lost Culture: The Brutal Legacy of Indigenous Schools," NYT, July 20, 2021; Thomas Fuller, "School Faces Founder's Role

in Native Killings," New York Times, October 28, 2021; Christine Chung, "At Nebraska School of Native Americans, a List of Dozens of Dead," NYT, November 18, 2021; Catherine Porter and Vjosa Isai, "Canada pledges $31.5 Billion to Settle Fight over Indigenous Child Welfare System," NYT, January 5, 2022.

143. Catherine Porter and Vjosa Isai, "Canada pledges $31.5 Billion to Settle Fight over Indigenous Child Welfare System," NYT, January 5, 2022.

144. New York Times, July 26, 2022.

Illustration Credits

Fig 1: Illustration. Source: *Arab Orthodox Christians Under the Ottomans 1516–1831* (Jordanville NY: Holy Trinity Publications) 2016. Scan: Holy Trinity Monastery.

Fig 2: Illustration. Source: *Miracles of St. Philaret Metropolitan of Moscow (1782–1867)* (Jordanville NY: Holy Trinity Publications) 2003. Scan: Holy Trinity Monastery.

Fig 3: Chromolithograph from the studio of I. and V. Morozov. Created from a photograph belonging to the Russian Ecclesiastical Mission in Jerusalem and taken in May 1887. Source: *"And I saw it with my own eyes": the 900th Anniversary of Igumen Daniel* (Moscow: Indrik) 2007. Scan: Holy Trinity Monastery.

Fig 4: Photograph. "В. Н. Хитрово." Source: http://www.antikbook.ru/interior/?bookshow1=2951, Public domain, via Wikimedia; commons.wikimedia.org/wiki/File: Хитрово_В.Н._ Русские_ Паломники_ Святой_Земли,_(1905).jpg

Fig 5: Photograph. "Tsar Alexander III" Source: *Великий Князь Сергей Александрович Романов на посту Председателя Императорского православного палестинского общества.* том IV (Москва : Новоспасский монастырь), 2011. Scan: Holy Trinity Monastery.

Fig 6: Lithograph. Studio of A. P. Zelenkov. “The Tomb of the Lord in the Holy City of Jerusalem.” Source: *And I saw it with my own eyes”: the 900th Anniversary of Igumen Daniel* (Moscow: Indrik) 2007. Scan: Holy Trinity Monastery.

Fig 7: Photograph. “Grand Duke Sergei Alexandrovich” Source: *Великий Князь Сергей Александрович Романов на посту Председателя Императорского православного палестинского общества.* том IV (Москва : Новоспасский монастырь), 2011. Scan: Holy Trinity Monastery.

Fig 8: Photograph. “Grand Duchess Elizabeth Feodorovna” Source: *Великий Князь Сергей Александрович Романов на посту Председателя Императорского православного палестинского общества.* том IV (Москва : Новоспасский монастырь), 2011. Scan: Holy Trinity Monastery.

Fig 9: Photograph. “On pilgrimage in Jerusalem.” Photographer: Monk Tikhon. Source: *Великий Князь Сергей Александрович Романов на посту Председателя Императорского православного палестинского общества.* том IV (Москва : Новоспасский монастырь), 2011 Scan: Holy Trinity Monastery.

Fig 10: “The Sergievskoe Compound in Jerusalem flying the IOPS flag” 1889. Source: *Великий Князь Сергей Александрович Романов на посту Председателя Императорского православного палестинского общества.* том III (Москва : Новоспасский монастырь), 2009. Scan: Holy Trinity Monastery.

Fig 11: Photograph: “The Sergei Courtyard.” 2020. Source: Boaz Rottem / Alamy Stock Photo, ID: 2B9A2E5.

Fig 12: Photograph. “Holy Trinity Cathedral” 1864. Source: *With the Russian Pilgrims to Jerusalem* by Stephen Graham (London: MacMillan and Co.) 1916. Scan: Holy Trinity Monastery.

Fig 13: Photograph. “The Municipal Hospital in the Russian Compound.” 1920. Source: Library of Congress, ID matpc.02579, via Wikimedia Commons, the free media repository.

Fig 14: Photograph. “The Russian school in Beit Jala” 1892. Source: https://www.researchgate.net/figure/The-Russian-school-in-Beit-Jala-1892-https-wwwipporu-historyippo_fig2_347774826. Creative Commons Attribution 4.0 International.

Fig 15: Photograph. “Four prominent members of The Pen League” 1920. Sources: rousseaustudies.free.fr/articleMcharek2006.html via commons.wikimedia.org/wiki/File:Algunos_miembros_de_Al-Rabita_al-Qalamiyya.jpg and alaraby.co.uk/sites/default/files/media/images/AD3D1D26-FB28-4D93-BDAE-ABBC20ED2D8F.jpg

Fig 16: Photograph: “Patriarch Gregory of Antioch.” Source: Prawoslavnaya Entsiklopediya, vol. XII, p. 607, Public domain, via Wikimedia Commons. commons.wikimedia.org/wiki/File:Patriarch_Gregory_of_Antioch.jpg

BIBLIOGRAPHY

Abū Ḥannā, Ḥannā, *The Russian Seminar of Nazareth, 1886–1914,* (Nazareth, 1994). (in Arabic).

Abū Ḥannā, Ḥannā, *The Vanguards of the Renaissance in Palestine, Graduates of Russian Schools,* 1862–1914, (Beirut, 2005). (in Arabic).

'Alī, Muḥammad K., *Khiṭaṭ al-Shām,* Vol. VI, (Damascus, 1928). (in Arabic).

Allen, Phillip C., *Spiridon and Meletios,* A Selection from Asad Rustum's *The Church of the City of God Great Antioch,* page 10, note 28.

Antonius, George, *The Arab Awakening,* Khayāts, (Beirut, 1938).

al-Aswad, Ibrāhīm, *The Enlightening of Minds in Lebanese History,* (Beirut 1935). (in Arabic).

al-'Aṭṭāwī, 'Abd al-Raḥīm, *al-Istishrāq al-Rūsī,* Center for Arab Culture, (Casablanca, 2002). (in Arabic).

Austen, Ian, "At Canada's Native Schools, a Grim Legacy of Cultural Erasure," (*New York Times,* July 6, 2021).

Balamand University, *The History of the Antiochian Orthodox Church,* (Lebanon, 1999).

Balamand University, *Russia and the Orthodox Christians of the East,* (Lebanon, 1998). (in Arabic).

Barker, A.J., *The War against Russia,* (Holt, Rinehart and Winston, New York, 1971).

Basili, Constantin M., *Syria, Lebanon, Palestine under Turkish Rule,* (Beirut, 1988). (Basili served as Russian Consul in Beirut from 1839–1853).

Bertram, Anton, *The Orthodox Patriarchate of Jerusalem,* Report of the Commission, (Oxford University Press, London, 1926).

Bliss, Frederich Jones, *The Religions of Modern Syria and Palestine,* (T.T.Clark, Edinburgh, 1912).

Callimachi, Ruckmini, "Lost Lives, Lost Culture: The Brutal Legacy of Indigenous Schools," (*New York Times,* July 20, 2021).

Campos, Michelle U., *Ottoman Brothers, Muslims, Christians, and Jews in Early 20th Century Palestine,* (Stanford University Press, 2011).

Chung, Christine, "At Nebraska School of Native Americans, a List of Dozens of Dead," (*New York Times,* November 18, 2021).

Dāghir, As'ad, *My Memoirs Regarding the Arab Cause,* (Cairo, n.d.). (in Arabic).

Dāghir, As'ad, "Russian Culture and Its Effect on Modern Arabic Literature," a lecture delivered in the 23rd Orientalist Convention in Moscow, 1960. (Reprinted from *al- Masarrah* magazine, no. 60, December 1979). (in Arabic).

Dāghir, Yūsuf A., "A Little Known Account in the History of Education in Syria, Lebanon and Palestine: The Imperial Palestinian-Russian Society," in *al-Adīb* Magazine, (January–February 1980): 16–19. (in Arabic).

Dāghir, Yūsuf A., *al-Madrasah al-Moskobiyya* (The Russian School), An Orthodox Christian Publication no. 3, al-Sā'iḥ Bookstore, (Tripoli, Lebanon, 1982). (a reprint in Arabic).

Ḍā hir, Masʿūd, *Beirut and Mount Lebanon about the Beginning of the 20th Century: A Study in Social History based on the Memoirs of Agafangel Krymsky (1871–1942),* (Dār al-Mada, Beirut, 1985). (A. Krymsky lived in Beirut and Mount Lebanon from 1896–1898). He was a Russian writer and scholar. (in Arabic).

Dreuzy, Agnes de, *The Holy See and the Emergence of the Modern Middle East: Benedict XV's Diplomacy in Greater Syria (1914–1922),* (Catholic University of America Press, Washington, DC, n.d.).

Eversley, G.J.S., *The Turkish Empire,* 1288–1924, (Howard Fertig, New York, 1969).

Faraḥ, Fu'ād, *The Living Stones, Arab Christians in the Holy Land,* (Nazareth, 2003). (in Arabic).

Field Jr., James A., *America and the Mediterranean World, 1776–1882,* (Princeton University Press, Princeton, 1969).

Finnie, David H., *Pioneers East,* (Harvard University Press, Cambridge, MA, 1967).

Fuller, Thomas, "School Faces Founder's Role in Native Killings," (*New York Times,* October 28, 2021).

Garrett, Mitchell B., and Godfrey, James L., *Europe since 1815,* (Appleton Century Crofts, New York, 1947).

Haddad, Robert, *Syrian Christians in Muslim Society,* (Princeton University Press, Princeton, 1970).

al- Ḥakīm, Yūsuf, *Beirut and Lebanon during the Ottoman Period,* (Beirut, 1964). (in Arabic).

al- Ḥakīm, Yūsuf, *Syria in the Ottoman Period,* (Beirut, 1966). (in Arabic).

al- Ḥakīm, Yūsuf, *Syria under Faisal I,* Memoirs no. 3, (The Catholic Press, Beirut, 1964). (in Arabic).

Ḥannā, George, *Before Sunset,* (Samya Press, Beirut, n.d.). (in Arabic).

Hawaweeny, Raphael, *A quick look at the History of the Greek Brotherhood of the Church of the Holy Sepulchre,* (Beirut, 1893). (in Arabic).

Ḥitti, Phillip, *The History of Lebanon,* (Beirut, 1985).

Hopwood, Derek, *The Russian Presence in Syria and Palestine 1843–1914: Church and Politics in the Near East,* (Clarendon Press, Oxford, 1969).

Horowitz, Jason, "Pope Makes His Frailty: A Lesson in Compassion," (*New York Times,* July 29, 2022).

Horowitz, Jason, and Ian Austen, "Pope Expresses Grief in Alberta over Brutality," (*New York Times,* July 26, 2022).

Hourani, Albert, *Arabic Thought in the Liberal Age, 1798–1939,* (Oxford University Press, 1967).

Hourani, Albert, *A History of the Arab Peoples,* (The Belknap Press, Cambridge, MA, 1991).

Jessup, Henry, *Fifty-three Years in Syria,* 2 Vol., (New York, 1910).

al-Kayyālī, Sāmī, *The Contemporary Syrian Literature, 1850–1950,* 2nd edition, (House of Knowledge (Dar al-Ma'arif), Egypt, 1968). (in Arabic).

Khālidī, Muṣṭafa, and 'Umar Farrūkh, *Preaching and Imperialism,* (Beirut, 1953). (in Arabic).

Khalīl, Osamah F., *America's Dream Palace,* (Harvard University Press, Cambridge, 2016).

Rev. Khallūf, Mīkhā'īl, *How I Became a Shepherd,* (Utica, New York, 1959).

Khleif, Walīd, and Suhayl Dyāb, editors, *Old Papers and Forgotten Correspondence,* (Nazareth, 1994). (in Arabic).

Kieser, Hans-Lukas, *Nearest East: American Millennialism and Mission to the Middle East,* (Temple University Press, 2010).

Krutz, Andrek, *Vatican Policy on the Palestinian-Israeli Conflict: The Struggle for the Holy Land,* (Greenwood Press, Westport, CT, 1990).

Kurbān, Met. Elias, *The Antiochian Patriarchal Crisis* 1891–1899, (Tripoli, 1979).

Kurbān, Met. Elias, *Memories (Kalimāt wa-Dhikrayāt),* (Lebanon, n.d.), p. 259. (in Arabic).

Lewis, Bernard, *The Emergence of Modern Turkey,* 2nd edition, (Oxford University Press, London, 1969).

al-Lliqā'al Orthothoksī (The Orthodox Encounter), *Russians in Lebanon Past and Present,* (Beirut, 2017). (in Arabic).

Makdisī, Usāma, *Artillery of Heaven,* (Cornell University Press, Ithaca, NY, 2008).

Mansel, Philip, *Aleppo: The Rise and Fall of Syria's Greatest Merchant City,* (I.B. Tauris, London and New York, 2018).

al-Nā'ūrī, 'Isa, *Adab al-Mahjar* [Place of Emigration] *The Literature of the Diaspora,* (Egypt, 1959). (in Arabic).

Nu'aimah, Mīkhā'īl, *Beyond Moscow and Washington,* (Ṣādir Press, Beirut, 1957). (in Arabic).

Nu'aimah, Mīkhā'īl, *Sab'ūn*: *The Story of My Life (1889–1959),* (Ṣādir Press, Beirut, 1959). (in Arabic).

Petkovitch, Constantin, *Lebanon and the Lebanese,* (Dār al-Mada Press, Beirut, 1986). (in Arabic). Translated from Russian to Arabic by Yūsuf 'Aṭallah, revised by Mas'ūd Ḍahir.

Porter, Catherine, and Vjosa, Isai, "Canada Pledges $31.5 Billion to Settle Fight over Indigenous Child Welfare System," (*New York Times,* January 5, 2022).

Povoledo, Elizabetta, and Austen, Ian, "Pope Hosts Canadians Who Request Apology for Indigenous Schools," (*New York Times*, March 29, 2022).

Richter, Julius, *A History of Protestant Missions in the Near East,* (Revell, Edinburgh and London, 1910).

Rijnekov, M., *Syria, Lebanon and Palestine, in the First Half of the Nineteenth Century,* (Al-Nahār Printing Press, Beirut, 1993). (in Arabic).

The Russian Presence in Palestine, (The Russian Ecclesiastical Mission in Jerusalem, Jerusalem, 1971).

Rustum, Asad, *History of the Church of Antioch,* III, 1453–1928, (Al Nur Publications, Beirut, 1928).

Rustum, Asad, *Lebanon in the Mutaṣarrifiyya Period,* (al-Nahār Press, 1973). (in Arabic).

Sa'īd, Edward W., *Out of Place: A Memoir,* (Knopf, New York, 1999).

Salībā, Najīb E., *Wilāyat Sūriyyā* (The Province of Syria, 1876–1909), (An unpublished doctoral dissertation, The University of Michigan, 1971).

al-Ṣalībī, Shaheen, *Images of Life,* al-Kitāb al-llubnanī, (Beirut, 1979). (in Arabic).

Stavrou, Theofanis George, *Russian Interests in Palestine, 1882–1914,* (Institute for Balkan Studies, Thessaloniki, 1963).

Swaidān, Shukrī Khalīl, *The History of the Imperial Orthodox Palestine Society,* (Boston, 1912). (in Arabic).

Tibawi, A.L., *American Interests in Syria,* 1800–1901, (Clarendon Press, Oxford, 1966).

Tibawi, A.L., *Arab Education in Mandatory Palestine,* (Luzac & Company, London, 1956).

Tibawi, A.L., *British Interests in Palestine,* 1800–1901, (Oxford University Press, 1961).

Tibawi, A.L., "The Genesis and Early History of the Syrian Protestant College," Part I, *Middle East Journal (MEJ),* 21:1, (Winter 1967), 1–15.

Tibawi, A.L., "The Genesis and Early History of the Syrian Protestant College," Part II, *Middle East Journal* (*MEJ*), 21:2, (Spring 1967), 199–212.

Tibawi, A.L., *A Modern History of Syria,* (St. Martin's, 1969).

Tibawi, A.L., "Russian Cultural Penetration of Syria and Palestine in the Nineteenth Century," *Journal of the Royal Central Asian Society,* Part II (1966), 53:3, 309–323.

Ṭūbī, Asma, *'Abīr wa-Majd,* (1966). (in Arabic).

Walker, Mark, "U.S. Report Details of Abuse of Native American Children at Federal Schools," (*New York Times,* May 12, 2022).

Yāghī, 'Abd al-Raḥmān, *Modern Palestinian Literature,* (Beirut, 1968). (in Arabic).

Zain, Nūr al-Dīn, *The Rise of Arab Nationalism,* (Beirut, 1968). (in Arabic).

Zaitūn, Joseph, *al-*Āsiyyah, 1840–1990, an unpublished study of education and schools in Syria. Al-Asiyyah was an Orthodox Christian Patriarchal School in Damascus. (in Arabic).

Ziadeh, Nicola, *Christianity and the Arabs,* (Cadmos Press, Damascus, 2000). (in Arabic).

Magazines and Papers

al-Adīb: A Literary Magazine (January–February 1980: 16–19), Beirut, Lebanon.

al-Funun, al-Sa'ih and al-Samir, were publications published by members of the Pen League [al-Rabita al-Qalamiyya which included famous Syrian writers in the U.S.]. In addition to being the voices of the League members, numbering about a dozen, they also contained a wealth of information and advertisements by Syrian merchants' businesses in the U.S.

Journal of the Royal Central Asian Society: 53:3.

al-Kalima: (The Word) The official publication of the Antiochian Orthodox Church in North America. It was founded in January 1905 and was published in Arabic. In 1957, English replaced Arabic.

al-Manār: (*The Lighthouse*) A religious publication which also covered scientific, cultural and educational news. (in Arabic).

al-Masarrah (Happiness): An Arabic newspaper which covered Syrian immigration issues.

The Middle East Journal (MEJ): Published by the Middle East Institute in Washington, DC. It covers Middle East news and developments since its foundation following WWII to the present.

al-Ni'ma: (*Grace*) was the official publication of the Antiochian Orthodox Patriarchate based now in Damascus, Syria. (in Arabic).

INDEX